CONTROLLING MERGERS AND MARKET POWER:
A Program for Reviving Antitrust in America

John Kwoka

Northeastern University

Competition Policy International, 2020

Copyright © 2020 by Competition Policy International
111 Devonshire Street · Boston, MA 02108, USA
www.competitionpolicyinternational.com
contact@competitionpolicyinternational.com

Printed in the United States of America

First Printing, 2020

Publisher's Cataloging-in-Publication Data provided by Five Rainbows Cataloging Services

Names: Kwoka, John, author.

Title: Controlling mergers and market power : a program for reviving antitrust in America / John Kwoka.

Description: 1st edition. | Boston : Competition Policy International, 2020. | Includes bibliographical references.

Identifiers: LCCN 2020930504 (print) | ISBN 978-1-950769-57-5 (paperback) | ISBN 978-1-950769-58-2 (hardcover) | ISBN 978-1-950769-59-9 (ebook)

Subjects: LCSH: Antitrust law. | Consolidation and merger of corporations. | Competition, Unfair. | Commercial law. | Law and economics. | BISAC: LAW / Antitrust. | BUSINESS & ECONOMICS / Mergers & Acquisitions.

Classification: LCC KF1649 .K86 2020 (print) | LCC KF1649 (ebook) | DDC 343.072/1--dc23.

Cover and book design by Inesfera. www.inesfera.com

CONTROLLING MERGERS AND MARKET POWER:
A Program for Reviving Antitrust in America

John Kwoka
Northeastern University

To Sarah

Foreword

John Kwoka's book, *Controlling Mergers and Market Power: A Program for Reviving Antitrust in America,* arrives at an opportune time: when a public debate has opened up over the appropriate contours of antitrust enforcement. It provides a thoughtful analysis of the problems with antitrust policy today, with an emphasis on merger control, and offers sensible recommendations for improvement.

Antitrust law was once exceedingly hostile to mergers. The mid-twentieth century Supreme Court, through landmark decisions like *Brown Shoe* and *Philadelphia National Bank*, blocked all but the smallest horizontal mergers (mergers between rivals). The courts of that era similarly erected high barriers to vertical mergers (mergers between firms and their suppliers or distributors).

The merger playing field changed substantially during the 1980s, though, when antitrust entered its Chicago school era. Under the influence of commentators associated with that approach, the appellate courts, in decisions like *Baker Hughes*, and the Reagan administration, in revising the Justice Department's Merger Guidelines, substituted a detailed economic analysis of merger harms and efficiencies for what had been rigid rules based on market structure.

The new approach facilitated influential methodological innovations in merger review—particularly the development of unilateral effects analysis—that likely improved the ability of the agencies and courts to discriminate between harmful and beneficial transactions. But it also allowed enforcers and courts to cut back on enforcement by ratcheting upward over time the concentration levels at which serious scrutiny of horizontal mergers set in, and by indulging Chicagoan presumptions that oligopolies usually perform competitively absent express collusion and that vertical conduct benefits competition.

Growing evidence, particularly from recent economic studies, indicates that the courts and agencies have relaxed antitrust enforcement, including merger enforcement, too far. Market power is on the rise in the U.S. economy, and overly lax merger enforcement is an important reason for this. In major industries where firms are exercising market power today, such as airlines and brewing, too many rivals have been allowed to combine. Vertical merger enforcement has also been neglected. One anecdote illustrates the problem. In 2018, a district court allowed a prominent vertical merger between a video programming provider (Time Warner) and a video distributor (AT&T, the owner of DirecTV) to proceed over the opposition of the Justice Department. This was the first vertical merger case litigated in decades. A year later, the merged firm notoriously and demonstrably raised its prices substantially—contrary to what the parties had represented in the proceedings and what the court predicted.

Deficiencies in merger enforcement have prompted increased scrutiny by federal and state authorities and by Congress. Legislative proposals have been introduced to increase deterrence of anticompetitive mergers by strengthening the hand of government and private plaintiffs in court. Even without new laws, John Kwoka explains in *Controlling Mergers and Market Power*, the enforcement agencies can and should do more.

Kwoka shows, using the FTC's own data on horizontal mergers, that the agencies have inappropriately narrowed their focus to mergers that come close to eliminating competition—mergers that leave a market with one, two, three, or perhaps four significant firms. That policy means that markets can change from a competitive structure to an oligopolistic structure without undergoing meaningful antitrust review. Kwoka also suggests that the enforcement agencies have become too accepting of efficiency claims, which acquiring firms systematically exaggerate.

Kwoka sensibly calls for rejuvenating the use of structural presumptions of harm arising from increased concentration, and looking carefully at mergers that today are scarcely given a second thought by agencies and courts. He also reasonably urges a greater enforcement focus on mergers that eliminate significant potential rivals, and on mergers, including vertical transactions, that would make it more difficult for fringe rivals and potential entrants to compete effectively. He appropriately calls for greater skepticism toward merging firms' efficiency claims, and for reviewing bodies to pay more attention to mergers that threaten innovation.

John Kwoka's previous book, a meta-analysis of all published merger retrospectives, highlighted the inadequacies of agency settlements. That book helped catalyze today's heightened attention to the shortcomings of merger control as it is currently practiced. Building on that work, Kwoka calls on enforcement agencies to accept fewer merger remedies, particularly conduct remedies, and instead to challenge mergers more often in court. His recommendations mainly target enforcement agencies, but he also properly recognizes that the agencies can't be effective without budgetary support from Congress. Starving agencies of resources is antitrust justice denied.

Acceptance of enforcement initiatives by the courts is also necessary for success in this endeavor—which makes the choice of cases to litigate a matter of great moment. The critical role of courts also leads Kwoka to recommend greater education of judges in modern competition analysis.

Controlling Mergers and Market Power makes a useful and timely contribution to this vital debate. It offers concrete proposals to make progress in addressing growing market power by providing a set of sensible analytical tools and concrete proposals for reform that are rooted in modern economic thinking. This is not surprising given John Kwoka's long and productive career as an industrial organization economist and his extensive scholarship on mergers and merger enforcement. It should be read and taken seriously by anyone interested in the contemporary policy debate about reinvigorating antitrust. And that most definitely includes the antitrust enforcers themselves.

Jonathan B. Baker

Preface

Until a few years ago, the problems associated with mergers and market power in the U.S. economy were topics debated and researched by a few economists and even fewer other observers. But the continuing consolidation of major industries plus the rise of dominant tech companies has prompted a growing number of conferences, white papers, legislative proposals, media articles, and reports. A watershed moment may have been the 2016 issuance of a policy brief from the Council of Economic Advisors expressing concern with these mergers and the state of competition in the U.S. economy.

Much research has now documented this merger wave and the resulting transformation of industries throughout the economy. These include airlines and drug stores, eyeglasses and hospitals, car rentals and agricultural seeds, dog food and industrial gases, beer and video entertainment, and countless more. As these changes have become widely recognized, a second phase of academic and policy research has delved into the causes and the effects of these mergers. Research has shown that one important cause has been a fundamental shift in merger enforcement by the U.S. antitrust agencies. My 2015 book *Mergers, Merger Control, and Remedies* (MIT Press, 2015) documented the increased permissiveness of antitrust policy over the past twenty-five years. It also compiled and reported new evidence of the adverse effects of these mergers on consumers and competition in the economy. Much additional research has reinforced these conclusions and concerns.

It is now time to move on to the next phase, which involves developing a comprehensive program of reforms of merger policy to address past weaknesses and equip it for the modern economy. Some reforms have been proposed and are under serious consideration, but these have tended to focus on specific issues that animate their advocates rather than addressing the full range of necessary changes. In addition, too much of what is being proposed does not take full advantage of constructive developments in antitrust economics, and indeed some proposals run counter to those developments.

The purpose of this book is to fill that void. It provides a comprehensive set of proposals to reform and revitalize merger control, covering the full extent of necessary changes, focusing on changes that are supported by modern antitrust economics and empirical evidence and informed by actual experience. In a very real sense, this monograph is a natural outgrowth of my earlier book. The purpose of *Mergers, Merger Control, and Remedies* was, as its subtitle indicated, to conduct "A Retrospective Analysis of U.S. Policy." The objective of this monograph is forward-looking: to provide a roadmap for reviving merger control, one that identifies the entire range of weaknesses of past policy, comprehensive in scope, rooted in the best available economic analysis and evidence, and capable of answering the ultimate question: What should we now do to strengthen merger policy and rein in market power in the economy?

In writing this book, I have benefitted from countless comments and suggestions that I have received in seminars, invited lectures, panel discussions, and other forums where I have presented aspects of this work. These include several American Antitrust Institute conferences and workshops, the American Bar Association Antitrust Section conferences, the CRESSE annual conference, the EU Directorate General for Competition, the Federal Trade Commission Hearings on Competition and Consumer Protection, the GCLC annual conference, Harvard Law School Antitrust Law and Economics seminar, International Competition Network conferences and workshops, the Mexican Competition Authority (COFECE), Northwestern University Searle Center Conference on Antitrust Economics and Competition Policy, the OECD Competition Commission meeting, the Peruvian Competition Authority (INDECOPI), the University of Chicago Antitrust and Competition Conference, and the Washington Center for Equitable Growth, among others. I am grateful to participants too numerous to mention.

I also want to thank staff at Northeastern University, especially Kathy Downey, for assistance with preparation of this manuscript, and my longtime colleague Larry White once again for his helpful input and advice. I am deeply grateful to Elisa Ramundo & Sam Sadden at Competition Policy International (CPI) for their interest in this manuscript, and for bringing it to fruition. And I want to give my special thanks to my partner Sarah Carleton for her unfailing support and assistance throughout this process.

Table of Contents

CHAPTER 1

Introduction

Some twenty years ago, then Assistant Attorney General Joel Klein declared, "Our economy is more competitive today than it has been in a long, long time."[1] Klein credited three forces for the state of competition at the time: sweeping deregulation of major industries such as airlines, energy, and telecom; growing foreign competition which revitalized the auto, steel, and other traditional domestic industries; and, of course, vigorous antitrust enforcement by both the Justice Department and the Federal Trade Commission. Regarding antitrust, he cited a number of major antitrust actions including price fixing cases, the successful challenge to Microsoft's monopoly, and tough scrutiny of mergers in airlines, accounting, and other industries.

Klein did not offer any statistical evidence about the state of economy-wide competition at the time, but considerable data have now emerged supporting his assessment of that period. Aggressive pursuit of mergers and Microsoft, together with challenges to price fixing and other conspiracies, had indeed reduced measured concentration and strengthened other metrics of competition in countless industries. But what Klein did not know, and of course could not have known, was that at the very moment he declared the economy to be characterized by historically strong competition, that competition had already peaked and begun to weaken. Measure after measure now shows that the steady rise in competition through the 1980s and 1990s had flattened out and begun a decline that has persisted to this day.

This reversal is evident in the very industries that Klein cited as examples of competition. Consider airlines: when Klein spoke, there were seven major airlines, but that number has dropped to four. The number of accounting companies has been cut in half, from eight to four. Sectors such as telecom and electricity were indeed deregulated, but since that time each has undergone massive consolidation. And if Microsoft were the monopoly prompting competitive concerns then, it has now been joined by four ad-

---

1 Joel Klein, Assistant Attorney General, Antitrust Division, U.S. Department of Justice, The Importance of Antitrust Enforcement in the New Economy, Address to the New York State Bar Assn. (Jan. 29, 1998).

ditional dominant companies—Amazon, Apple, Facebook, and Google—sitting astride key sectors of the economy: internet search, social media, smartphones, and e-commerce.

These are not isolated examples. In industry after industry, large and small, prominent and less well known, consumer-oriented and producer-oriented, numerous studies have documented a substantial increase in concentration since the 1990s. These include brewing, supermarkets, car rentals, hospitals, dog food, eyeglasses, industrial chemicals, cable TV, agricultural chemicals, crop seeds, medical equipment, home laundry equipment, wireless carriers, meat packing, mobile home manufacturing, mattress manufacturing, and veterinary clinics, among many others.

Most of these increases in concentration have now been widely noted, but the more fundamental problem lies in the harmful effects of concentration on competition, consumers, and businesses. Studies have demonstrated that this rise in concentration has already resulted in higher prices, persistent abnormal profits, reduced investment and innovation, and declining rates of firm start-up, entry, and growth. These are the metrics of competition, and they are in sharp decline. They have already resulted in harm to our economy and pose a growing threat to its future health and strength unless actions are taken, and taken now.

But what actions? The answer to that question requires understanding the causes of rising concentration and its linkage to competition. Several factors have played a role, but a major cause has been the growing permissiveness of antitrust policy over the past twenty to thirty years. This permissiveness is clear from the history of approved mergers in the ever more concentrated industries listed above. It is also reflected in the ever narrower grounds on which the antitrust agencies have come to challenge mergers, limiting efforts to prohibit mergers to the most egregious cases. And it is embodied in the agencies' increasing determination to devise what they claim are remedies to mergers rather than bringing necessary challenges, remedies that often prove ineffective.

This overall permissiveness has had widespread effects throughout the economy, but it takes on special significance in the tech sector. The five major tech firms have acquired more than 600 companies, some of which would likely have evolved into rivals to their dominance or at least limited their extension into other sectors. Out of these hundreds of acquisitions, there has been exactly one court challenge, and that one was settled with a remedy of doubtful effectiveness. In addition, practices that insulate these companies from present or future competition are much less often challenged than in the era of *Microsoft*. Indeed, one wonders whether that case might even be brought at the present time.[2]

By the mid-2000s, the retreat of antitrust policy had become so evident that the Wall Street Journal—the consummate business press—opined that "The federal government has nearly stepped out of the antitrust enforcement business, leaving companies to mate as they wished."[3] Even allowing for a bit of journalistic hyperbole, this observation is a startling recognition of the profound changes in antitrust policy and practice since the 1990s. From its origins as a "comprehensive charter of economic liberty aimed at preserving free and unfettered competition,"[4] from its role in achieving a nearly unprecedented degree of competition at the time of Klein's assessment, antitrust has since that time presided over a sweeping consolidation of U.S. industry. Mergers that, in the words of a recent Attorney General for Antitrust, "should never get out of the boardroom"[5] have increasingly come to be proposed because they have too often been approved by the agencies or in the courts.

In the face of this record, it is not an exaggeration to conclude that recent antitrust policy has failed in its mission of "preserving free and unfettered competition." And it is no exaggeration also to conclude that actions to restore competition are necessary and urgent, and those actions require fundamental reforms of antitrust policy and practice. It is the purpose of this book to set out a comprehensive plan for how to reform and revive antitrust policy, focusing on the issue of mergers.

---

2 In an interesting parallel, the FTC investigated but then closed its case against Google for biasing search results toward its own or favored sites based on arguments that could have been used to justifying closing the *Microsoft* case fifteen years earlier. Statement, U.S. Federal Trade Commission, Statement of the Federal Trade Commission Regarding Google's Search Practices, (January 3, 2013). Documents indicate that decision to close was opposed by key FTC staff. Brody Mullins, Rolfe Winkler & Brent Kendall, *Inside the FTC Probe of Google*, WALL STREET JOURNAL, Mar. 19, 2015. See also Richard Gilbert, "The U.S. Federal Trade Commission Investigation of Google Search," in THE ANTITRUST REVOLUTION (J. Kwoka & L. White, eds., 7th ed. 2019).

3 Dennis Berman, *How to Assess 2007 M&A Activity*, WALL STREET JOURNAL, Jan. 16, 2007.

4 Supreme Court opinion in *Northern Pacific Railway v. United States*. 356 U.S. 1, 4 (1958).

5 Comment by Assistant Attorney General for Antitrust William Baer, American Bar Assn, Antitrust Section meetings, Washington DC, April 2015. Reported in Brent Kendall, *As Mergers Multiply, U.S. Antitrust Cops Raise Their Game*, WALL STREET JOURNAL, July 2, 2015.

Even among those who broadly agree with this critical assessment of antitrust policy, there is a wide spectrum of proposed policy alternatives. Some advocate one or two specific policy changes—greater attention to the tech sector or to agriculture, for example, or perhaps increased resources for the antitrust agencies. At the other end of the spectrum are those who view the entire intellectual and policy framework of antitrust as deficient and urge its replacement with a far broader mandate, including attention to such factors as income inequality, the sheer size and political power of large corporations, workers' rights, and environmental considerations, and so forth.

Most of these proposals reflect a deep frustration with the role of recent antitrust policy and practice. This book shares that deep frustration, but it will argue—and demonstrate—that the measures necessary to restore antitrust are neither the small tweaks that some have proposed, nor the complete overthrow of the current framework advocated by others. Rather, the recommendations herein represent a comprehensive package of very substantial reforms that collectively would transform antitrust policy, restoring its vitality and thereby putting it back on course to achieve its fundamental mission of ensuring competition.

The specific recommendations herein derive from close economic analysis of the deficiencies of current policy. Indeed, we begin by analyzing precisely what has gone wrong—that is, what types of mergers are mistakenly being approved. We then analyze the reasons for those erroneous policies. Once those are identified, we then draw on relevant economic evidence and policy experience to explain the changes in policies and practice that are necessary to address each of these issues.

The result is a broad and deep plan for reforming merger policy and practice. To be sure, some specific reforms have already been proposed and discussed in many recent forums and papers, but the reform program proposed here is different in two important respects. First of all, rather than advancing one or two proposals, it is a fully comprehensive program. It consists of a full array of specific substantive reforms as well as some procedural reforms. Moreover, while each reform has merit, this package is an integral whole rather than a menu of alternatives among which to choose. One cannot, for example, advocate that the agencies undertake more merger investigations without considering the need for more resources or urge that they make greater use of the structural presumption without resolving empirical questions of thresholds. In short, merger control is an integrated, multifaceted policy, and hence this package of necessary reforms is also an integral whole.

Secondly and importantly, this package of proposals is firmly rooted in modern economic theory and empirical evidence. The proposals are not simply interesting or seemingly sensible ideas—though, at a minimum, they surely are that. Nor is each the result of some isolated experience or observation. Rather, each follows from current economic understanding of market competition and market failure, from compilations of data and statistical testing, and from lessons learned from the practical application of antitrust economics to policy. Indeed, each recommendation will be accompanied by a precise justification and citation to supporting economic evidence. The interested reader can then follow the trail of evidence, gaining a better understanding of the contributions—and some limitations—of economic research to antitrust policy and practice.

To set the stage for this plan, we begin with two preliminary issues. One is the eroding state of competition in the U.S. economy. Evidence for this forms the foundation for the remaining discussion, since it highlights the specific concerns with competitiveness of the economy as a whole. The second preliminary issue involves the erosion of merger control in recent years. Here we explain the forces that have altered merger policy and led to the current permissive stance. This, too, is a necessary step towards the recommendations that follow.

The actual program covers twelve substantive areas plus three process matters that also require reforms. The substantive areas and recommendations are, in brief, as follows:

(1) The Merger Guidelines: The agencies must begin to strictly enforce their own Horizontal Merger Guidelines as written. This would reverse a longstanding trend toward practices that increasingly deviate from the nominal standards of enforcement.

(2) The Structural Presumption: Merger policy should place greater reliance on a presumption that certain high-concentration mergers are essentially always anticompetitive. This would avoid having to develop the same degree of case-specific proof when other evidence suffices.

(3) Efficiencies: The agencies need to adopt a more skeptical view of merging firms' claims of efficiencies and other benefits from mergers. Compelling economic evidence indicates that significant offsets rarely occur and should equally rarely be counted in favor of a merger.

(4) Ease of Entry: The agencies should avoid accepting routine claims that entry is sufficiently easy to discipline existing firms except where, by evidence of past entry or documented intent, the possibility of entry can be indisputably established.

(5) <u>Impediments to Entry</u>: Antitrust needs to challenge mergers that create barriers to new entry and the growth of small firms. This would be a significant addition to the current focus on shorter-term competitive harms, such as immediate price effects.

(6) <u>Potential Competition</u>: The agencies should restore prominence to the economically sound doctrine of potential competition. This doctrine states that mergers eliminating a significant potential competitor can be anticompetitive.

(7) <u>Nonprice Effects</u>: The agencies must evaluate more closely mergers for their possible anticompetitive effects on important nonprice outcomes. These include quality, service, costs, and perhaps most significantly, innovation.

(8) <u>Monopsony</u>: The agencies need to address the anticompetitive potential of buyer market power—"monopsony"—in markets where a merger results in only one or a few buyers of some product or service. This competitive problem has been almost entirely overlooked.

(9) <u>Remedies</u>: The agencies must sharply limit the use of remedies, especially conduct remedies, as alternatives to challenges to anticompetitive mergers. These remedies have been shown often to be ineffective in preventing competitive harms.

(10) <u>Vertical Mergers</u>: Mergers between firms at successive stages of production can be methods for exercising or extending market power at either stage. Enforcement must be more attentive to this possible competitive harm and more aggressive in challenging such mergers.

(11) <u>Common Ownership</u>: There is legitimate concern over diminished competition in markets where financial firms have ownership stakes in major competing firms. More research is necessary in order to establish operational criteria for agency actions.

(12) <u>The Tech Sector</u>: The tech companies have been engaged in large numbers of unchallenged mergers and acquisitions, some fraction of which raises competitive concerns. These need to be viewed much more carefully and critically.

With respect to the antitrust enforcement process, three specific areas are the focus of recommendations. These are as follows:

(1) <u>Retrospective Studies</u>: The agencies should routinely conduct retrospective studies of the outcomes of past mergers and their own policies

toward them. Such studies would help inform the agencies about the effectiveness of their enforcement decisions and policies.

(2) <u>Resources</u>: The increasing demands on the antitrust agencies require more resources in order for them to conduct necessary investigations and challenges. Over many years, their resources have shrunk relative to workload and not even kept up with inflation.

(3 <u>Judicial Education</u>: The judiciary must be educated in modern competition analysis in order to be better able to evaluate and judge the cases brought before them. At present, too many economically unsound decisions make their way into case law.

With this outline in mind, the next two chapters examine our two foundational questions—the state of competition in the economy, and the evolution of merger control policy.

CHAPTER 2

THE ERODING STATE OF COMPETITION IN THE U.S. ECONOMY

In April 2016, the President's Council of Economic Advisors ("CEA") issued a brief on the state of competition in the U.S. economy. It cited "several indicators suggest[ing] that competition may be decreasing" and offered some possible explanations for the decline.[6] One of those explanations was weakness of competition policy. The CEA Brief was a milestone in the public debate about competition in the U.S. economy and the role of policy, but it was scarcely the only such discussion or document. Both before and after that brief was issued, a number of studies and reports had been examining these issues, and a number had suggested that antitrust policy indeed bore at least some responsibility for the changes in concentration and competition.[7]

The purpose of this section is not simply to review those studies, since there now are a number of good summaries of that literature.[8] Rather, the purpose is to formulate the issues and evidence in terms of the underlying

---

6 Council of Economic Advisers (2019), *The Benefits of Competition and Indicators of Market Power*, (April 2016), https://obamawhitehouse.archives.gov/sites/default/files/page/files/20160414_cea_competition_issue_brief.pdf.

7 Prominent among these are Jonathan Baker, THE ANTITRUST PARADIGM (Harvard University Press, 2019); Thomas Philippon, THE GREAT REVERSAL (Harvard University Press, 2019); and Jonathan Tepper, THE MYTH OF CAPITALISM (Wiley, 2019).

8 See, for example, *A National Competition Policy*, AM. ANTITRUST INST. (September 28, 2016) https://www.antitrustinstitute.org/wp-content/uploads/2018/08/AAINatlCompPolicy-1.pdf. Jonathan Baker, *Market Power in the U.S. Economy Today*, WASHINGTON CENTER FOR EQUITABLE GROWTH, (March 20, 2017), https://equitablegrowth.org/market-power-in-the-u-s-economy-today/; Jay Shambaugh, Ryan Nunn, Audrey Breitwieser, Patrick Lu & Becca Portman, *16 Facts about Competition and Dynamism*, BROOKINGS, (June 2018), https://www.brookings.edu/research/the-state-of-competition-and-dynamism-facts-about-concentration-start-ups-and-related-policies/; *Carl Shapiro, Antitrust in an Age of Populism*, 61 INTERNATIONAL JOURNAL OF INDUSTRIAL ORGANIZATION, 2018.

economics of competition. That involves, first, identifying the characteristics of a competitive market and then, second, organizing the empirical evidence in terms of those characteristics. This approach provides a sounder basis for our conclusion about the state of competition than, as do some reports, simply observing increases in concentration or high profits, and then drawing some conclusions. It also serves as a foundation for the specific policy recommendations in the subsequent sections, making clear that they follow from the underlying economics of markets and competition.

This framework is built on three economic propositions that define and determine competitive market operation. These are as follows:

(1) A competitive market is characterized by a substantial number of sellers and buyers, with due allowance for any economies associated with size.

(2) In competitive markets, entry and growth of new firms, and exit of existing firms, should be relatively easy, free of obstacles, and therefore common.

(3) Profits in competitive markets should be at normal levels, except for temporary deviations due to market disequilibria.

These three propositions highlight characteristics of a well-functioning market—low/moderate concentration, ease of entry, and normal profits—and, where they do not hold, that indicates diminished competition.[9] Thus, if firm numbers decline and concentration rises over time, absent evidence of changes in underlying economies, that would represent an indication of weakening competition since the remaining fewer firms would become more capable of a variety of anticompetitive actions and strategies. Entry and growth (and exit of weak or inefficient firms) represent market responses to economic opportunities and changed conditions, responses that restore competition where it has weakened. If, however, these normal responses are impeded or do not occur, that would signify declining dynamism and competitiveness of these markets. And if profits are excessive and persistent, that would suggest some combination of fewer incumbent firms, inadequate entry, and anticompetitive strategies. Together, evidence supporting these three factors would lead inescapably to the conclusion that competition has diminished.

What follows is a brief summary of the voluminous evidence on these three issues—concentration, entry, and profits.

---

9 In strict economic terms, either large numbers of agents or very free entry might suffice, but normally both are essential for good market operation.

2.1 Rising Concentration

Ideal concentration data would be at the rather detailed level of the economic or antitrust market, but such data are not generally available. As a result, most studies and research have had to settle for either more aggregated measures in order to get comprehensive coverage of industries, or alternatively, more precise measures but on a modest number of sectors. The originally cited CEA contained some of both types of evidence: it referenced detailed studies of rising concentration in a few fairly well-defined sectors—hospitals, wireless carriers, and rail transportation—but it also reported data on the rising revenue share of the top 50 firms in two-digit sectors.[10]

The implications of the CEA Brief have been corroborated by a number of other reports measuring changes in concentration on a more disaggregated basis. *The Economist* collected data on more than 900 sectors of the U.S. economy and reported that over a fifteen-year period concentration had increased in two-thirds of them.[11] Figure 2.1 is based on data in that report, summarizing evidence by sector. While the average concentration levels across most sectors remained modest, that study reported that the total revenue shares of the more concentrated sectors have grown most rapidly. This implies that overall concentration has been rising faster than the average suggests, since the increase is greater in the larger and more concentrated sectors.

---

10 It acknowledged that both the two-digit sectoral level ("transportation and warehousing") and the top-fifty firm aggregation were overly aggregated. Critics have erroneously pounced on this table as if the conclusions in the CEA Brief rested entirely on it.

11 *Too Much of a Good Thing: Profits Are Too High. America Needs a Giant Dose of Competition*, THE ECONOMIST, March 26, 2016.

FIGURE 2.1

Top Four Firms' Average Share of Total Revenue, %

United States, across 893 industries, grouped by sector*

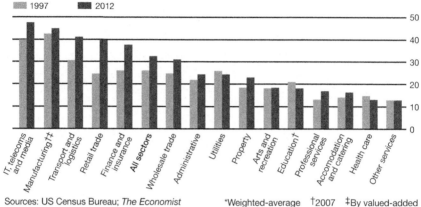

Sources: US Census Bureau; *The Economist*   *Weighted-average   †2007   ‡By valued-added

Autor et al.[12] have examined nearly 700 industries in the U.S. economy and have found that since 1987, concentration has broadly increased in manufacturing, finance, services, wholesale and retail trade, and utilities. Their findings are robust to alternative measures of concentration and also to controls for import competition. Grullon et al.[13] study publicly traded companies in the U.S. and report that measured concentration in fact declined during the 1980s and into the 1990s. Beginning in the late 1990s up through 2014, however, they find that concentration rose for three-quarters of all sectors, and by an average of 50 percent, from which they conclude there has been "a structural shift in US product markets that has weakened competition."[14] More recently still, the Open Markets Institute has issued a study of rising concentration in more than thirty markets and sectors of the U.S. economy, in most cases again finding dramatic increases.[15]

---

12 David Autor, David Dorn, Lawrence Katz, Christina Patterson & John Van Reenen, *Concentrating on the Fall of Labor Share*, 107 AMERICAN ECONOMIC REVIEW 5, 180-85, (2017).

13 Gustavo Grullon, Yelena Larkin & Roni Michaely, *Are U.S. Industries Becoming More Concentrated?* 23 REVIEW OF FINANCE 4, 697–743, 2019.

14 This pattern is precisely that noted above in conjunction with Klein's 1999 statement about overall competition in the U.S. economy.

15 *America's Concentration Crisis*, OPEN MARKETS INSTITUTE, (Nov. 2018), https://concentrationcrisis.openmarketsinstitute.org/.

As noted, none of these datasets or studies is perfect. Each represents a different trade-off between detail and coverage. Some are at broader sectoral levels (for example, 3-digit industries) in order to capture more of the overall economy, whereas others are at a more granular level but then for fewer industries. All, however, arrive at the same essential conclusion: measured concentration has been steadily and broadly increasing throughout U.S. markets at least since the late 1990s. There is no evidence that this conclusion is the result of imperfect data. Nor is there any indication that it has been the result of widespread changes in economies of scale, apart, of course, from certain tech and platform companies. And it is also noteworthy that there appear to be no studies showing the contrary, that concentration in the U.S. economy has in fact been decreasing during this time.[16]

Some observers have called for further data collection and analysis before drawing conclusions about economy-wide trends in concentration. There is no doubt that more and better data would be useful, but any recommendation for further study before taking action is effectively a prescription for postponing action indefinitely. A study at the level of what are known as "antitrust markets" would require examination of hundreds of thousands of such markets, since antitrust markets are typically very narrow in both their product and geographic dimensions.[17] Moreover, examining even a small fraction of those markets would require data that resides with the antitrust agencies and not with outside researchers. The Antitrust Division of the Justice Department and the Federal Trade Commission have data from past investigations that might be brought up to date. In addition, the FTC has the legal authority to require companies to provide data more broadly.

Interestingly, the FTC once used that authority to compile such data. From 1975 to 1984, that agency's Line of Business Program required most of the 500 largest companies to provide considerable data on their operations

---

16 In their recent study, Rossi-Hansberg et al. document a divergence between national and local concentration that appears to be due to entry by national firms such as Walmart into numerous local markets. By definition that lowers local market concentration until a new equilibrium is reached, which the authors show can take several years. See Esteban Rossi-Hansberg, Pierre-Daniel Sarte & Nicholas Trachter, "Diverging Trends in National and Local Concentration," April 2019.

17 Several examples prove the larger point. In the *Steris-Synergy* merger, the antitrust market was defined as "contract sterilization of medical devices, pharmaceuticals, and other products." In the *Staples-Office Depot* proposed merger, the market was "consumable office supplies sold through office superstores" in each city or parts thereof. In the *US Airways-American* airline merger, the Justice Department listed hundreds of city-pair "antitrust markets" where competition was arguably affected. These examples are typical.

and finances in relatively narrow "lines of business." The program was intended to help identify performance outliers across sectors and over time, in an effort to develop common metrics of corporate structure and performance and also to facilitate antitrust scrutiny of markets. The FTC's experience was telling: Data collection was vigorously opposed by corporate interests and their allies in Congress and was terminated after four years.[18] The antitrust agencies have shown no inclination to restart any such program.

Thus, rather than focusing on the lack of perfect data, the better question is whether the present evidence, taken as a whole, provides sufficiently convincing support for the proposition that concentration has been increasing steadily and significantly. Indeed, that is the case, and there is sufficient reason for action now even as efforts at further data collection proceed.

2.2 Declining Entry Rates and Aging Firms

Higher concentration might logically be a transient phenomenon, one that takes care of itself by attracting new firms to enter and smaller firms to grow. The end result of that process would be the restoration of competition in these markets. But the evidence for the U.S. economy contradicts that possibility and instead finds that most markets are characterized by reduced rates of entry and declining populations of firms. The CEA Brief displayed firm entry and exit rates in the U.S. economy between 1980 and 2010. Based on the Census Bureau's Business Dynamics Statistics and reproduced here as Figure 2.2, this chart shows in dramatic fashion that while firm exit rates remained roughly constant over this period, the firm startup rate has been in long-term decline. In recent years the pace of that decline has picked up speed, with the startup rate falling by half over the past ten years or so.

---

18 See David J. Ravenscraft & Curtis L. Wagner, *The Role of the FTC's Line of Business Data in Testing and Expanding the Theory of the Firm*, 34 THE JOURNAL OF LAW & ECONOMICS 2, 703–39 (1991).

FIGURE 2. 2

Firm entry and exit rates, 1980-2010

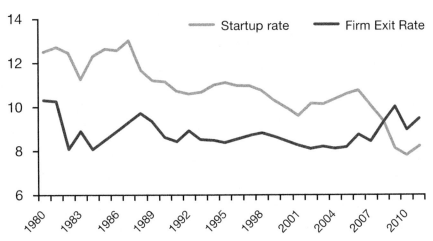

Sources: Council of Economic Advisors (2016)

Numerous studies corroborate this finding. Decker et al.[19] report that the decline in startup rate characterizes virtually all sectors of the economy, including—most recently—the tech sector. They also study the impact of "young" firms, defined as those less than five years old, and find that over the past thirty years such firms account for a declining share of all firms, new jobs created, and total employment in the economy. Shambaugh et al. report that while firms less than ten years old accounted for 33 percent of employment in 1987, that percentage fell to 19 percent by 2014. They further document the sharp decline in firm start-up rates across all sectors during this period.[20]

A recent study by Doidge et al.[21] finds that the number of publicly traded firms in the U.S. economy peaked in the mid-1990s and has been falling ever since, by nearly 50 percent. It is now down to the level of the 1970s when the economy was roughly one-third its present size. That long-term decline is depicted in Figure 2.3 here.

---

19 Ryan Decker, John Haltiwanger, Ron Jarmin & Javier Miranda, *The Role of Entrepreneurship in US Job Creation and Economic Dynamism*, 28 JOURNAL OF ECONOMIC PERSPECTIVES 3, 3-24 (2014).

20 Jay Shambaugh, Ryan Nunn, Audrey Brietwieser, Patrick Lu & Becca Portman, *16 Facts about Competition and Dynamism*, BROOKINGS 2018.

21 Craig Doidge, Kathleen Kahle, G. Andrew Karolyi & Rene Stulz, *Eclipse of the Public Corporation or Eclipse of the Public Markets?* (NBER, Working Paper No. 24265; 2018).

FIGURE 2.3

Declining population of public firms:
Numbers, 1982-2012

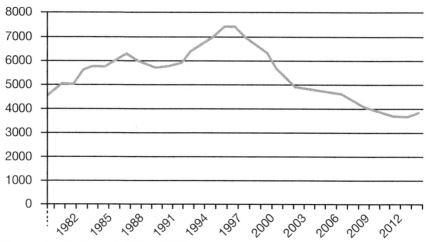

Sources: Council of Economic Advisors (2016)

They further report that the decline in firm numbers has been especially severe for small firms (they term it a "collapse"), resulting in a sharply higher average age of publicly listed firms. Whereas at the peak the average age was twelve years, that had risen to twenty years by 2016. Moreover, in a finding that foreshadows analysis in our next chapter, that study finds that 61 percent of disappearances of publicly traded firms since 1997 has been due to mergers, again an increase from prior years.[22]

These studies are in full agreement both in terms of their broad conclusions and with respect to important details. It seems clear that the late 1990s marked the high point for firm entry and numbers, after which a steady decline in both metrics of competitive dynamism set in. This timing is also consistent with the previously cited data on rising concentration since the 1990s—and with Klein's favorable assessment of competition in the U.S. economy in 1998.

What is less immediately clear is the cause of these changes in entry, exit and firm numbers. Comprehensive data on entry decisions, entry barriers, and other possible contributing factors across numerous industries simply do not exist. There is, however, considerable evidence of the rise of barriers to

---

22 Further evidence is the fact that the Wiltshire 5000 Index no longer consists of 5000 qualifying public companies. Rather, it can only find about 3500 companies.

entry in a number of important sectors. These include some industry-specific practices that inhibit entry and growth of smaller rivals, such as various distribution practices in brewing and soft drinks,[23] pay-for-delay agreements in generic drug introductions,[24] shelf space allocation methods in supermarkets and other retailing,[25] patenting practices and standards setting in the tech sector,[26] takeoff and landing rights ("slots") in airlines,[27] most favored nation clauses in video programming and other markets,[28] and many others. Some other impediments to entry are less sector-specific. These include the greater difficulty of entry in the face of vertical integration (thus requiring multi-level entry by any competitor), network effects (which can confront small-scale entry with very low strategic pricing by incumbents), and the increasingly important role of data as a critical input into a number of markets.[29] Anecdotally, such impediments seem to have grown in number and importance in recent times, perhaps as firms recognize their long-term advantages.

One sector where there is good statistical evidence of the recent harmful rise in entry barriers is in various professional occupations. While entry into some occupations is justifiably limited by training requirements, certification,

---

23 Tripp Mickle, *Craft Brewers Take Issue with AB Inbev Distribution Plan*, WALL STREET JOURNAL, Dec. 5, 2015. *Diane Bartz, Justice Department Investigates Beer Industry Anticompetition Accusations*, REUTERS, Oct. 12, 2015.

24 See Michael Salinger, Pauline Ippolito & Joel Schrag, *Economics at the FTC: Pharmaceutical Patent Dispute Settlements and Behavioral Economics*, 31 REVIEW OF INDUSTRIAL ORGANIZATION, 85-105 (2007). Also, Joseph Farrell & Mark Chicu, *Pharmaceutical Patents and Pay for Delay: Actavis*, in THE ANTITRUST REVOLUTION 7th ed., (John Kwoka & Lawrence White eds., 2019).

25 Among many analyses, see for example Leslie Marx & Greg Shaffer, *Slotting Allowances and Scarce Shelf Space*, 19 JOURNAL OF ECONOMICS AND MANAGEMENT STRATEGY 3, 575-603 (2010).

26 For further discussion, see Marc Jarsulic, Ethan Gurwitz & Andrew Schwartz, *Toward a Robust Competition Policy*, CENTER FOR AMERICAN PROGRESS, (April 3, 2019), https://www.americanprogress.org/issues/economy/reports/2019/04/03/467613/toward-robust-competition-policy/. Consistent with this, Grullon et al. report that the year 2000 signaled a change in the statistical relationship between concentration and patenting activity. Starting in that year, the relationship became positive, which they interpret as suggesting that "technological barriers to entry may have prevented new firms from entering profitable markets."

27 Susan Stellin, *Seeking a Place at Airports*, NEW YORK TIMES, Jan. 25, 2010.

28 Jonathan Baker & Fiona Scott Morton, *Antitrust Enforcement Against Platform MFNs*, 127 YALE LAW JOURNAL, 2176-2202 (2018).

29 With respect to network effects, see Victor Aguirregabiria & Chun-Yu Ho, *Hub-and-Spoke Networks and Entry Deterrence*, 28 INTERNATIONAL JOURNAL OF INDUSTRIAL ORGANIZATION 4 (2010).

and licensing, that cannot be said of the strict licensing requirements imposed by some states on businesses such as florists, upholsterers, fortune tellers, beekeepers, chimney sweepers, junkyard dealers, turtle farmers, and rainmakers.[30] In these cases licensing is transparently a device to prevent entry.

The CEA Brief reported that the fraction of workers in the economy covered by occupational licensing has risen dramatically, from about 4 percent in the 1950s to nearly 30 percent by 2008. In addition to occupational licensing, non-compete agreements, no-poaching and no-hiring agreements, non-disclosure requirements, and other restrictions on labor mobility and entry represent growing impediments into various professions and occupations.[31] While these restrictions seem most common in the occupations, they are not unique to that setting.

All of these factors create or enhance obstacles to entry and growth, and interrupt the normal adjustment process of markets. A great many of these appear to be the direct result of deliberate efforts by firms to insulate themselves from competition from new or smaller firms.

2.3 Rising and Persistent Profits

If both concentration and entry barriers have risen significantly, as the evidence indicates, this would suggest a decline in competition. Critical evidence for or against this prediction would be data showing that profits have risen to, and persist at, above normal levels. That is indeed what a range of evidence, including from several sources already referenced, shows. For example, the same issue of *The Economist* that reported on rising concentration also observed that profits as a fraction of GDP in the U.S. have risen to nearly an all-time high, as has return on capital adjusted for goodwill.[32] It further reported that profits were not only larger but ever more persistent. A firm with a high rate of return on capital in 2003 had an 83 percent chance of still being very profitable a decade later, an increase from only 50 percent ten years earlier. "The obvious conclusion is that the American economy is too cozy for incumbents," it concluded.[33]

---

30 For a more extensive list of 50 that are licensed in every state, see Adam Summers, *Occupational Licensing*, REASON FOUNDATION (August 1, 2007), https://reason.org/policy-study/occupational-licensing-ranking/.

31 For discussion, see Randy Stutz, *The Evolving Antitrust Treatment of Labor Market Restraints: From Theory to Practice*, AM. ANTITRUST INST, (July 31, 2018). Also, Alan Krueger & Orley Ashenfelter, *Theory and Evidence on Employer Collusion in the Franchise Sector* (NBER, Working Paper No. 24831, 2018).

32 *The Economist*, op. cit.

33 *Ibid.*

Similarly, the Grullon et al. study finds firm profitability to have risen over time, with most of that increase in concentrated industries starting around 2001.[34] They find the source of excess profits to be higher price-cost margins rather than efficiencies. Shapiro reports census data showing that over the past thirty years the fraction of GDP due to profits has risen by 50 percent, from 7-8 percentage points to 11-12 percent. The latter figure represents an all-time high.[35] Figure 2.4 illustrates this trend. De Loecker & Eeckhout's analysis of price-cost margins comes to a similar conclusion. As shown in Figure 2.5, they report that price-cost margins in the U.S. economy have grown continuously and rapidly after 1980, contributing to widespread increases in prices.[36] Jarsulic et al. adopt a different measure, namely, the ratio of the market value of a company to the replacement cost of its capital.[37] This ratio, commonly called Tobin's Q, captures investors' expectation of excess profit, and their data show that this measure has increased—albeit irregularly—since about 1980 and has become much more persistent for individual firms.

FIGURE 2.4

Corporate Profits as Percent of GDP 1985 to 2016

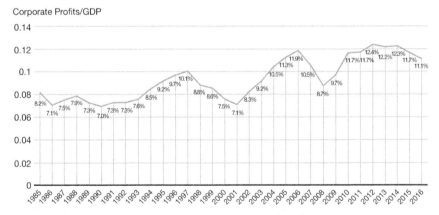

Source: Bureau of Economic Analysis, Table 1.7.5, "Relationship of Gross Domestic Product, Gross National Product, Net National Product, National Income and Personal Income," Last Revised September 28, 2017, available at https://bea.gov/iTable/iTable.cfm?reqid=19&step=2#reqid=19&step=3&isuri=1&1910=x&0=9&1921=survey&1903=43&1904=1977&1905=2017&1906=a&1911=0

---

34 Grullon et al., op cit. Some of their variables are imperfectly measured, weakening the conclusion.

35 Shapiro, op. cit.

36 Jan De Loecker & Jan Eeckhout, *The Rise of Market Power and the Macroeconomic Implications* (NBER, Working Paper No. 23687, 2017).

37 Jarsulic et al., *supra* note 26.

FIGURE 2.5

Sales-weighted Average Markups (1960 – 2014) in U.S. Economy

Sources: De Loecker & Eeckhout (2017)

Some other studies have investigated further questions such as the distribution of high profits, their persistence, and the role of mergers. The CEA Brief reported that return on capital for a typical firm at the 90th percentile was more than five times the median, whereas twenty-five years earlier it was only twice as large.[38] Doidge's study finds that overall profits in the market are now divided among fewer winners than ever before and that more of the accounting profit accrues to firms whose core asset is intellectual property.[39] Blonigen & Pierce specifically examine the role of mergers and find that they result in higher profit margins rather than gains in productivity, compared to otherwise similar non-merging firms.[40]

The clear implication of these many studies is that, by our best measures, profits in U.S. industries are unusually large, have been growing, and

---

38 CEA.

39 Doidge et al., *supra* note 21.

40 Bruce Blonigen & Justin Pierce, *Evidence for the Effects of Mergers on Market Power and Efficiency* (Finance and Economics Discussion Series 2016-082. Washington: Board of Governors of The Federal Reserve System, 2016).

are ever more concentrated in fewer large firms.[41] While the data have limitations—notably, the difference between accounting and economic profit—the better studies perform corrections and sensitivity tests whenever possible. All nonetheless continue to find the same basic results.

2.4 Implications for Competition and Competition Policy

This review of the evidence establishes that concentration, entry impediments, and profits in the U.S. economy have each been rising. A great many of the studies find that these trends started in the mid- to late- 1990s, lending credence to the proposition that they are rooted in a common phenomenon. Furthermore, as noted in the initial discussion of the economic framework, these results on concentration, entry, and profits are more than three separate findings, although of course they are of independent interest. More importantly, they test and confirm a causal linkage from concentration and entry impediments directly to excess profit and an erosion in competition. Put differently, while each finding might have some alternative explanation, there is no convincing alternative to all three of them jointly—no explanation, that is, other than that competition in the U.S. economy has been in decline.

Moreover, while each individual study has its limitations, the various studies corroborate and reinforce each other. Each draws on somewhat different data, overlapping in some cases, closing gaps in others, and adding to the cumulative body of evidence arriving at the same conclusion. It is, in short, the totality of the evidence that is conclusive.

This assessment of the state of competition raises the question of the role and responsibility of recent merger policy and practice. This will be the subject of analysis in the next chapter.

---

41 Corporate profits are directly affected by tax laws, among other factors. The recent $1.5 trillion tax cut directed at corporations and high-income individuals has produced a corporate windfall and furthered the stock market boom. See James Mackintosh, *The Fed Worries about Corporate Monopolies, Investors Should Just Buy Them*, WALL STREET JOURNAL, Aug. 24, 2018.

CHAPTER 3

THE EVOLUTION–AND EROSION–OF MERGER CONTROL

Merger control in the United States is guided by a statutory prohibition on consolidations whose effect "may be substantially to lessen competition, or to tend to create a monopoly."[42] Over the past one hundred years, interpretation of this standard has evolved, reflecting the dominant issues of the time, economic understanding of competition, and political and ideological forces. The original interpretation of the statute by the courts and the Justice Department in the 1960s led to an aggressive structure-based policy, one that found competitive threats even in mergers of fairly modest size. Those original stringent standards and enforcement practices have few, if any, advocates now. Over time, however, the bar for approving mergers has been progressively lowered past some intermediate position to the point that mergers of quite substantial size in concentrated industries are being approved. Indeed, this trend seems to have accelerated over the past twenty years or so, contributing to the rise in concentration and decline in competition in the U.S. economy described in the last chapter.

This chapter will begin by documenting this transformation of merger policy from one that was overly stringent to the current permissive version. There is considerable evidence for this trend, including data from the agencies themselves, on their actual merger control practice. Other evidence corroborating this narrowing of merger enforcement includes the progressive relaxation of the formal standards for problematic mergers in the agencies' own Horizontal Merger Guidelines and independent assessments of the state of enforcement.

This analysis of merger control policy and practice will be followed by an enumeration of the forces that have contributed to this evolution—and indeed erosion—of merger control. These include the rise of *laissez-faire* ideology and, paradoxically, some subsequent economic advances intended to challenge that ideology by providing an alternative approach. These analyses will form the foundation of our recommendations for the reform of merger control.

---

42 Clayton Act (1914), as amended.

3.1 The Horizontal Merger Guidelines

As previously noted, the original 1968 version of the Merger Guidelines articulated a stringent standard for a competitively problematic merger. It defined a "highly concentrated market" as one where the four-firm concentration ratio exceeded 75 percent, and stated that, for example, a merger between two 4-percent firms in that market would "ordinarily" be challenged as anticompetitive. While that reflected a common view of the over-riding importance of concentration at the time, the specific thresholds were soon seen as unsupportable.

The next iteration of the Merger Guidelines, issued in 1982, is generally regarded as the first "modern" version. It relied on the same two-criteria decision framework—the level of concentration and the size of merging firms (as measured by the change in concentration due to the merger)—but the new thresholds were quite different, as, indeed, was the index of concentration. The latter was the HHI, calculated as the sum of the square of market shares of all firms in the antitrust market.[43] These new guidelines defined a high concentration industry as one with HHI in excess of 1800 (the equivalent of nearly six equal size firms, or more likely about eight firms with typical size variation). The guidelines flatly stated that "The Department is likely to challenge mergers in this region that produce an increase in the HHI of 100 points or more"—a statement widely viewed as a presumption that such a merger would elicit a challenge. These guidelines also provided for somewhat lower likelihood of challenge for mergers that either raised HHI by less or arose in less concentrated industries, or both. In addition, the guidelines sought to allay concern about enforcement actions against mergers deemed unlikely to be problematic. It established what came to be known as a "safe harbor" for a merger of any size in a "low concentration" industry, defined as one with HHI less than 1000 (ten equal size firms). Here, the guidelines stated, "the [Justice] Department is unlikely to challenge mergers falling in this region."

The basic framework of the 1982 guidelines remained the operative version for nearly thirty years,[44] during which time free market advocates

---

43 Since HHI reflects both firm numbers and the variation in their shares, a convenient interpretation of HHI is "numbers-equivalent" —the number of equal size firms that would result in a particular value. The numbers equivalent is calculated as 10,000/X, where X is a particular observed value. Thus, an HHI of 2000 could result from a market with five equal size firms. This interpretation should be used with caution since no actual industry is made up of equal size firms. In reality an HHI of 2000 would likely be made up of 7 or 8 firms of moderately varying size.

44 There was a significant revision in 1992, as well as minor revisions in 1984 and 1997. The important change in 1992 was the introduction of the unilateral effects theory of mergers, as will be discussed below.

successfully pressed for ever looser interpretation of these standards. They argued that concentration did not imply market power, that entry was sufficiently easy, that efficiencies were common, and that policy overall was too strict. The result was that actual agency enforcement deviated from the announced guidelines to an ever greater degree. Indeed, the 2010 revision of the Merger Guidelines was said not to represent new policy but rather simply to reflect actual practice.[45] Those new 2010 Guidelines significantly loosened the parameters of merger control policy in several ways. The thresholds for a merger raising competitive concern became an industry with HHI greater than 2500 and an increase of at least 200 points. An HHI of 2500 implied an industry with four exactly equal-size firms, down from nearly six in the previous guidelines, and a change of 200 points would involve two 10-percent firms, up from two firms each with 7 percent share. As shown in the comparison illustrated in Figure 3.1, these changes served to exclude a considerable range of mergers that previously would have received close scrutiny.

FIGURE 3.1

Thresholds for Likelihood of Merger Challenges
1992 and 2010 Merger Guidelines

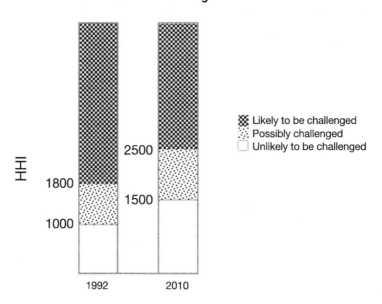

---

45 Christine A. Varney, Assistant Att'y Gen., Antitrust Div., Dep't of Justice, An Update on the Review of the Merger Guidelines, Remarks as Prepared for the Horizontal Merger Guidelines Review Project's Final Workshop (Jan. 26, 2010), https://www.ftc.gov/sites/default/files/documents/public_events/horizontal-merger-guidelines-review-project/100126transcript.pdf.

Moreover, the characterization of competitive concerns and the likelihood of a challenge changed as well. As noted, the 1982 Guidelines stated that the Justice Department was "likely to challenge" a merger exceeding its thresholds, whereas the 2010 Guidelines stated only that a merger exceeding its (now looser) thresholds "will be presumed to be likely to enhance market power." A "presumption of a likelihood" would seem to convey a lesser degree of certainty than the earlier "presumption of a challenge," especially when, as the 2010 Guidelines immediately went on to note, "The presumption may be rebutted by persuasive evidence showing that the merger is unlikely to enhance market power."

And finally, these new guidelines greatly enlarged the range of mergers in the "safe harbor." Whereas in the earlier version, that line was set at an HHI of 1000, the 2010 Guidelines raised that to 1500 (approximately seven equal-size firms). This represented a substantial expansion of the safe harbor, as evidenced by the fact that the new HHI threshold of 1500 was almost as high as the level that previously defined a high concentration industry—1800. That is, the previous point where any sizeable merger was viewed as likely to be challenged was only slightly greater than the new level where any merger was altogether unlikely to be challenged. The major policy shift embodied in these guidelines could not be more stark.

3.2 Merger Control in Practice

These changes did not go unnoticed in the economic, policy, and legal communities. Among the notable studies, Baker & Shapiro reported on two different analyses of changes in the agencies' enforcement practices. First, they compiled and updated data for the period 1982 through 2007 on the percent of proposed mergers filed under the Hart-Scott-Rodino Act that were challenged by the two antitrust agencies.[46] Subject to some caveats, they observed a low level of enforcement during the 1980s, followed by a reversion to historically more typical levels during the 1990s. Subsequently, they reported that "merger enforcement during the current [2002-2007] administration has been surprisingly low, particularly at the Antitrust Division." Indeed, by the time of the last data available to them (2006-07), the rate had fallen "below the lowest level previously recorded." Baker & Shapiro calculated that, at something like historic average rates,

---

46 Jonathan Baker & Carl Shapiro, Reinvigorating Horizontal Merger Enforcement, in HOW THE CHICAGO SCHOOL OVERSHOT THE MARK, (R. Pitofsky, ed., Oxford, 2008). As defined in the underlying data, a challenge includes, in addition to formal complaints and litigation, mergers resolved by remedies and those abandoned by the parties in the face of agency opposition. The authors report that data for 1982-2001 were taken from a previous compilation by FTC Commissioner Thomas Leary.

the two agencies would have challenged a remarkable total of about 24 additional mergers per year.

This conclusion was corroborated by these authors' second assessment. This was based on a survey of twenty "experienced antitrust practitioners" in Washington, DC, regarding their views of then current merger policy at the Justice Department and the FTC. They reported that these practitioners rated merger review at both agencies "significantly more receptive to arguments made by merging parties" with a "sharply higher" likelihood of "successful agency review for the merging parties" compared to ten years earlier. The respondents further reported that this accommodating view affected all stages of the enforcement process from second requests, to likelihood of closure of an investigation, to weaker remedies.

This fundamental change in merger enforcement is conclusively documented by data released by one agency on its own enforcement practice. This dataset covers all the FTC's merger investigations over the 16-year period 1996 through 2011, and reports the number of investigations and the number of enforcement actions according to various firm and industry criteria.[47] By focusing on mergers with specific characteristics, these data controlled for the possibly changing mix of mergers over time—one of Baker & Shapiro's concerns—and thereby avoided misinterpreting what might simply be a changing mix of merger types as an actual policy change.

Table 3.1 here reports the percent of investigations that resulted in any type of enforcement action, according to the number of remaining significant competitors in the market. A "significant competitor" is defined by the FTC as "a firm whose independence could affect the ability of the merged firms to achieve an anticompetitive outcome,"[48] or loosely, a "firm that matters." Recall that a market with HHI of 2500—termed highly concentrated—must have at a minimum four significant competitors if they are of exactly equal size, and as a practical matter more like six or seven when their sizes vary.

---

47 United States Federal Trade Commission. 2013. "Horizontal Merger Investigations Fiscal Years 1996-2011." No comparable data is available for the DOJ Antitrust Division, and indeed, the FTC has ceased releasing updates. According to the report, "enforcement actions" are decisions to take action against a merger, but includes cases where parties to a merger abandoned the transaction.

48 FTC, 2004, n. 42. This number is a convenient single criterion that reflects both the level of and the merger-related change in concentration. The FTC report also contains tabulations of investigations and enforcement actions based on HHI and its changes that are fully consistent but somewhat less easy to interpret.

TABLE 3.1

Merger Investigations Resulting in Enforcement Decisions

Number of remaining significant competitors	Percent enforced				
	1996-2011	1996-2003	2004-2005	2006-2007	2008-2011
1	98.0	96.2	100.0	100.0	98.4
2	89.2	84.8	89.3	94.7	95.7
3	77.3	76.1	50.0	86.7	91.9
4	64.1	61.5	57.1	69.2	72.7
5	35.2	40.6	28.6	44.4	0.0
6	12.0	20.0	16.7	0.0	0.0
7	24.0	50.0	0.0	0.0	0.0
8	0.0	0.0	0.0	0.0	0.0
Total	78.6	77.0	78.7	70.8	89.0

Source: Federal Trade Commission, Horizontal Merger Investigations data, Fiscal Years 1996-2011 (Jan. 2013) available at https://www.ftc.gov/sites/default/files/documents/reports/horizontal-merger-investigation-data-fiscal-years-1996-2011/130104horizontalmergerreport.pdf.

The first column in Table 3.1 reports that percentage of investigations resulting in enforcement actions by the number of remaining significant competitors over the entire 16-year period. As one might expect (and certainly hope), the likelihood of an enforcement action rises systematically as the number of remaining significant competitors declines. Mergers, for example, that resulted in five remaining competitors triggered actions about 35 percent of the time—not an overwhelming fraction, but indicating significant enforcement activity. Mergers with fewer remaining competitors had actions taken with correspondingly greater frequency.

The remaining columns of this table break these percentages down by four subperiods that can be identified from the sequence of FTC reports: 1996-2003, 2004-2005, 2006-2007, and 2008-2011.[49] Two implications of these data are of critical importance. First, for mergers resulting in one or two or three or even four remaining competitors—that is, mergers in very high concentration markets—the likelihood of enforcement action remains high over time. For mergers to monopoly, for example, the percent subject to enforcement action has varied in the narrow range between 96 and 100

49 These subperiods are determined by the somewhat irregular release dates for the FTC data compilations. Each was cumulative from 1996 to its nominal date. By taking differences in totals, differences in percentages over time can be calculated.

percent. For those with two, three, or four remaining competitors, the percent has in fact increased over time by about 10 percentage points, although the level of enforcement for four remaining competitors—72.7 percent—diverges considerably from the others. Yet overall, for these four categories, the percent subject to enforcement is substantial.

An entirely different pattern, however, characterizes mergers resulting in more than four remaining competitors. In each case, the likelihood of enforcement action has systematically—and precipitously—declined. For those resulting in five remaining competitors, for example, the percent triggering any enforcement action fell from over 40 percent during the period from 1996 to 2003, to 29 percent in 2004-2005, then ticking upward to 44 percent before falling to literally zero thereafter. A similar pattern is evident for mergers resulting in six and seven significant competitors, but in each case the decline started sooner and fell to zero in an earlier interval—by 2006-2007 for six competitors, by 2004-2005 for seven competitors. Indeed, the regularity of this pattern—illustrated in Figure 3.2—makes clear that merger enforcement had been undergoing systematic retrenchment.

FIGURE 3.2

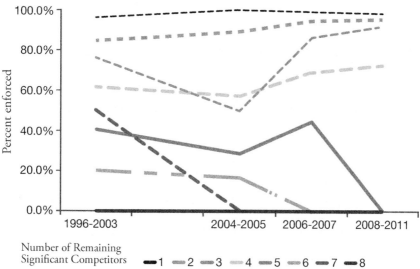

Percent of Agency Investigations that Were Enforced

Sources: Author's calculations based on FTC (2013)

Indeed, not just retrenchment: by 2008, the likelihood of any type of enforcement action—even a negotiated remedy or abandonment in the face of threatened action—for any merger with more than four remaining competitors had fallen to literally zero. That is, merger enforcement against all mergers in this moderately high to high concentration category had literally ceased, sending a green light to companies contemplating a merger of this sort. And as indicated by the previously quoted Wall Street Journal article, that green light shone clearly to all: "the federal government has nearly stepped out of the antitrust enforcement business."[50]

This evidence—the agency's own data, with its chosen market definitions, based on its internal records of decisions and actions, and fully comprehensive for a sixteen-year period—leaves no doubt about the profound changes that merger enforcement has undergone in the past twenty years. And the consequences of this profound shift in policy are predictable: abandoning merger enforcement against such mergers can only lead to the rise in concentration in market after market.

3.3 Origins of Merger Policy Change

How did a change of this magnitude and importance come about? Was it accidental or deliberate? Was it the result of one administration or political party, or not? Did it reflect considered policy or more effective advocacy? The origins of this policy shift are important to understand. It answers an obvious question concerning a change in a major domestic policy that occurred at a slow enough rate as to escape much attention until recently, but that cumulatively has had profound effects on the structure and competitiveness of the economy. Beyond that, understanding its origins constitutes the foundation for a plan to revive merger control policy by addressing the very policies that collectively have led to the present state of weakness.

While a number of forces have combined to produce this radical shift in merger policy, the major causes are twofold. Many observers would likely—and rightly—point to the rise of the Chicago school of Economics in the 1970s as a major driving force behind this policy shift. That school challenged the "structural" view of competition that resulted in the stringent 1968 Merger Guidelines and some controversial antitrust cases at the time. The Chicago School argued that, to the extent that market structure mattered at all, it was only one of many factors and not by itself a reliable predictor of competition. Indeed, its advocates contended that larger market shares and high concentration were more likely indicators of firm efficiency and product superiority rather than market power. Consequently, they argued that there were greater risks and costs from errors of commission—challenging harmless or procompetitive practices—than from errors

---

50 Op. cit.

of omission in which harmful practices are tolerated. The overall result was that true competition problems were viewed as infrequent and that antitrust policy should have a correspondingly limited role.

Much of this view was articulated by Robert Bork in his landmark treatise *The Antitrust Paradox.* Bork in fact advocated a sweeping transformation of antitrust, asserting that it should "abandon its concern with such beneficial practices as small horizontal mergers, all vertical and conglomerate mergers, vertical price maintenance and market division, tying arrangements, exclusive dealing and requirements contracts, 'predatory' price-cutting, price 'discrimination,' and the like."[51] With respect to horizontal mergers, his position was clear: only those resulting in monopoly or duopoly should be challenged. Three firms should be sufficient for a competitive market.

Despite the fact that virtually every one of Bork's specific claims has been shown to be incorrect or limited by unrealistically strong assumptions,[52] his views had enormous impact. The succession of merger guidelines and merger enforcement practices reflects Bork's position. The broad and skeptical perspective toward mergers in the early versions of the guidelines was replaced with a less structure-based and more accommodating approach. Efficiencies and entry were formally incorporated as defenses, criteria for each were provided, and claims welcomed. The mechanism of competitive harm from any merger would need to be specified rather than presumed, and if it could not be explained, the concern was unlikely to be sustained. To be sure, some of these changes have been meritorious, even essential, in order to ensure that enforcement practices reflect modern industrial organization. But the collective effect of these changes was to significantly narrow the antitrust mission.

But another development has contributed to the evolution of a narrow merger control policy. That development—ironically—has been the so-

---

51 Robert Bork, THE ANTITRUST PARADOX: A POLICY AT WAR WITH ITSELF (1978).

52 Jonathan Baker, *Taking the Error Out of 'Error Cost' Analysis: What's Wrong with Antitrust's Right,* 80 ANTITRUST LAW JOURNAL, 1-38 (2015). The success of Bork's views was aided by the Chicago School's routine rejection of contrary evidence. As described by Melvin Reder, "Chicago School economists tend strongly to appraise their own research and that of others by a standard which requires...that the findings of empirical research be consistent with the implications of standard price theory." He goes on to describe any "apparent inconsistency" as "anomalous" and requiring, first and foremost, a "re-examination of the data to reverse the anomalous findings." Melvin Reder, *Chicago Economics: Permanence and Change,* JOURNAL OF ECONOMIC LITERATURE, 1-38 (1982).

called (and awkwardly named) "post-Chicago" school. This latter is less of a school or coherent program than a series of theoretical developments and empirical findings that have pushed back on the Chicago school's simplistic models and provided a sound basis for restoring certain aspects of merger policy. The problem with these "post-Chicago" advances is that, while correct and now quite widely accepted, they have addressed rather specific issues, so that progress against the *laissez-faire* ideology has been very uneven. The result has been that, without an overall framework, these specific advances have resulted in other equally meritorious concerns being overlooked and, by contrast, seeming even weaker.

One example of this scenario involves the threshold task of establishing the "antitrust market." In order to demonstrate competitive harm from a merger, the Merger Guidelines define an antitrust market as a set of products whose price can be increased by a "small but significant and nontransitory" amount. This has followed from sound underlying economics, directing attention to specific product markets of concern and often leading to successful challenges to mergers. At the same time, however, it has resulted in several unfortunate outcomes. One is that it has elevated price effects—where the economic model and tools are most powerful—to a pre-eminent position even if other concerns—such as quality or innovation—are of equal, and sometimes greater, importance. Furthermore, it has often turned merger analysis into narrow econometrics-driven exercises attempting to measure factors such as diversion ratios, critical loss analysis, and upward pricing pressure into various economic models of pricing.

Moreover, this approach has often led to exceedingly narrow market definitions, such as those noted in Chapter 2, and narrowly defined markets have had further adverse effects. For one, they often place certain possible providers of substitute products—firms not producing the product but with the potential to enter under some circumstances—outside the antitrust market. That in turn has resulted in greater ease for an incumbent firm to acquire such an outside "potential competitor" since it is not a direct competitor and accordingly is less likely to be challenged. That is unfortunate since the elimination of such a potential competitor removes an immediate threat to the inside firm and in the longer term prevents that outside firm from evolving into a true rival by entering and bringing direct competition to bear on the incumbent firm. As we shall also see, this has been one factor contributing to the very large number of tech company acquisitions of seemingly unrelated firms that have gone unchallenged.

Another problem that follows from a narrow market definition concerns remedies to mergers, and in particular divestitures. If a merger of two multiproduct firms involves a competitively problematic overlap in only one product, that issue can often be resolved simply by requiring divestiture of one of the two overlapping operations or products to a third party that has no overlaps. But what constitutes such a qualifying third party depends upon the definition of the market: a narrower definition results in more "nearby" firms being technically not in the market and hence qualifying as potential buyers of the divested product or assets, even if they are in fact not entirely unrelated. Again, the point is that the evolution of this important and successful policy tool—market definition—has rendered both remedy policy and potential competition mergers more difficult to implement.

3.4 Reviving Merger Control

This review has made several things clear: there has been a dramatic shift in merger policy over the past twenty-five or so years; this shift has been the direct and indirect product of several forces; and this shift has fed directly into the rise in concentration and the decline in competition in the U.S. economy. With this as background, we now turn to the question of what needs to be done to reverse this trend, to restore a vigorous merger control policy, and thereby to strengthen competition in markets throughout our economy.

What follows is a series of topic areas—fifteen in all—that require reform. For each we provide an analysis of current policy and practice, setting out its flaws and limitations. This is followed by specific recommendations for reforms that will revive merger control. We begin with the role of market structure in merger control.

CHAPTER 4

RE-ESTABLISHING THE ROLE OF MARKET STRUCTURE: Merger Guidelines and the Structural Presumption

This chapter focuses on the key—and controversial—issue of the appropriate role of market structure in merger analysis and the weight to be attached to it. As previously noted, market structure has been a particular focus of the Chicago school critique, as a result of which the importance of market shares and concentration in merger review has substantially diminished over time. This has been despite convincing and, indeed, mounting evidence of the relevance of these factors.

This chapter first examines the degree to which the antitrust agencies enforce their own standards for market structure as stated in the Horizontal Merger Guidelines. We shall review data from the antitrust agencies themselves showing that their enforcement practices fall systematically short of those standards, and indeed, by a greater margin over time. We then go on to examine evidence of the importance of market structure in predicting the outcomes of actual mergers. That evidence supports considerably greater reliance than presently attributed to market structure. Each of these sections concludes with specific recommendations for strengthening merger enforcement based on this evidence.

4.1 Enforcement of the Horizontal Merger Guidelines

Each version of the Merger Guidelines sets out a framework for analyzing horizontal mergers based on then-current economic understanding. As noted, the specific standards for what constitutes a competitively problematic merger have changed over time, from the quite stringent thresholds of 1968, to the more moderate standards of 1982, and now to the further relaxed criteria of 2010. But whatever the standards have been at any point in time, actual practice has generally been more permissive than those stated guidelines. Most of the enforcement action has in fact been in a range of concentration significantly higher than the apparent criteria for a competitively problematic merger. This failure to enforce the written standards has contributed directly to the rise in concentration and decline in competition in numerous markets.

Evidence of this permissiveness comes from an unimpeachable source—the agencies' own data. Key evidence is data published by both the FTC and the DOJ Antitrust Division describing characteristics of all the antitrust markets where the two agencies challenged mergers in the years 1999-2003.[53] As context, we note that the Horizontal Merger Guidelines operative at the time stated that any merger raising HHI by more than 100 and where the market HHI would exceed 1800 was likely to be challenged. Somewhat lesser probabilities of challenge applied to mergers where either the level of or the change in concentration was more modest.

The agencies' data show clearly that there were relatively few challenges to mergers near those thresholds; rather, the vast majority of challenges were to mergers at considerably higher levels of concentration and share changes. Table 4.1 is a tabulation from the FTC-DOJ report showing the frequency of merger challenges in markets with various levels of HHI concentration and of merger-related increases in HHI concentration. As shown, during this time, the agencies challenged in some fashion mergers involving 1263 distinct product and geographic markets, arising from a total of 173 mergers. It is immediately apparent that relatively few mergers—only about 14 percent—were subject to challenge in markets with HHI less than 2500, and even fewer at an HHI below 1800. Indeed, the lowest HHI for any challenged merger was said to be about 1400, while the median was an astonishingly high 4500-5000. At this level there would typically be only two similar size firms in the post-merger market. That is, nearly half of all challenges were to the extreme cases of mergers to duopoly, and only one-half involving mergers at any lesser level of concentration.

---

53   FEDERAL TRADE COMMISSION AND DEP'T OF JUSTICE MERGER CHALLENGES DATA (2004). https://www.ftc.gov/sites/default/files/documents/reports_annual/merger-challenges-data-1999-%E2%80%93-2003/mdp_0.pdf. These data have been compiled and reported in useful forms in John Kwoka, MERGERS, MERGER CONTROL AND REMEDIES: A RETROSPECTIVE ANALYSIS OF U.S. POLICY (MIT Press, 2015, hereafter *MMCR*).

TABLE 4.1

Count of Markets in which the Agencies Challenged Mergers (1999-2003)

Post-Merger HHI	Change in the HHI								
	0-99	100-199	200-299	300-499	500-799	800-1,199	1,200-2,499	2,500+	total
0–1,799	0	17	18	19	3	0	0	0	57
1,799–1,999	0	7	5	14	14	0	0	0	40
2,000–2,399	1	1	7	32	35	2	0	0	78
2,400–2,999	1	5	6	18	132	34	1	0	197
3,000–3,999	0	3	4	16	37	63	53	0	176
4,000–4,999	0	1	3	16	34	30	79	0	163
5,000–6,999	0	2	4	16	9	14	173	52	270
7,000+	0	0	0	2	3	10	44	223	282
total	2	36	47	133	267	153	350	275	1263

Source: Federal Trade Commission and Department of Justice 2004

The gap between agency practice and the guidelines standards is even more clear when HHI data are analyzed in combination with the change in HHI. While the guidelines provide that a merger is very likely to be challenged when HHI is at least 1800 and the change in HHI exceeds 100, Table 4.1 shows—rather remarkably—that there were exactly two such cases out of 1263 mergers investigated during this period. In addition, only for those mergers where HHI rose by 300-499—well beyond the nominal standard of 100—were there many investigations resulting in challenges.

These data make clear that agency enforcement focused on mergers with much greater concentration levels and changes than stated in the Merger Guidelines. Corroboration for this conclusion comes from the FTC's Merger Investigations Data that were described and analyzed in Chapter 3 above. That dataset showed that merger enforcement between 1996 and 2011 in practice was much more permissive than the stated guidelines, that enforcement became ever more permissive over this period, and indeed that enforcement ultimately ceased for a broad swath of mergers supposedly subject to challenge under the stated guidelines.

These actual data from the agencies, in short, make clear that the standards articulated in the Merger Guidelines have generally borne only a loose relationship to actual enforcement practice, and indeed, less of a relationship over time. This gap between standards and practice has not been a mistake. Rather, the standards have twice been loosened, most recently in 2010, and the rationale is telling. According to the then-Assistant Attorney General for Antitrust, the rationale in 2010 was to close "the gaps between the Guidelines and actual agency practice,"[54] specifically citing the fact that the agency no longer challenged mergers with HHIs and changes near their respective lower boundaries. The speciousness of this rationale is clear: If actual practice is unduly permissive, it is doubling down on that error to change stated policy in the guidelines to conform to erroneous practice. Rather, the burden should fall on agency practice to strengthen enforcement at that margin.

Compounding that error, loosening the standard will likely simply result in a new gap between that standard and actual enforcement. The practical reason is that the standard is never a bright-line. Rather, prospective merging firms close to that border are more likely to proceed with their merger, and the agency is less likely to prevail against it, than in the case of a merger with characteristics classifying it as more problematic. To that extent, shifting the boundary will simply result in a new group of mergers at that new boundary and a new apparent "gap" between the stated standard and actual practice. Shifting the boundary simply results in a never-ending cycle and an ever more permissive standard.[55]

It should be noted that the concentration thresholds set forth in the Merger Guidelines are geared primarily to one theory of harm from mergers, namely, "coordinated effects." This theory focuses on the greater likelihood that the post-merger industry, with one fewer firm, will succeed in coordinating pricing and other strategies. Such coordination is the traditional concern with mergers, and of course there is good economic evidence that firm numbers do affect that likelihood. Over the past twenty-five years, however, much attention has been paid to the alternative theory of harm from a merger known as "unilateral effects." In this theory, a merger between firms selling imperfectly substitutable products is more likely to raise prices to the extent that each firm in raising its own price would lose some sales to the other firm. The merger recaptures those otherwise lost sales, making a price rise more profitable. The unilateral effects approach has been increasingly relied upon by the FTC since its introduction in the 1992 Merger Guidelines. By one

---

54 Christine A. Varney, Assistant Att'y Gen., Antitrust Div., Dep't of Justice, An Update on the Review of the Merger Guidelines, Remarks as Prepared for the Horizontal Merger Guidelines Review Project's Final Workshop (Jan. 26, 2010), https://www.ftc.gov/sites/default/files/documents/public_events/horizontal-merger-guidelines-review-project/100126transcript.pdf.

55 For evidence of the change in proposed mergers when the standard changes in an analogous setting, see Thomas Wollman, *Stealth Consolidation: Evidence from an Amendment to the Hart-Scott-Rodino Act*, 1 AER INSIGHTS, 77-94, (2019). See also Lawrence White, Why Isn't "Deterrence" Included in the Measurements of Antitrust "Enforcement"?, CPI ANTITRUST CHRONICLE, Nov. 2019, Vol. 2(2), pp. 66-70.

analysis,[56] whereas cooperation and collusion were alleged in more than half of challenges in 1989-90, that fraction fell to between 20 and 40 percent for 1993-2005, and under 15 percent thereafter. In short, unilateral effects have come to comprise a substantial majority of concerns with mergers.

Market concentration and firm shares are less central to unilateral effects cases. Formal analysis of the latter rests primarily on the closeness of substitutes and the margins on the goods in question rather than traditional market structure criteria. To that extent, any gap between standards and practice is more subtle and difficult to establish for mergers analyzed for their unilateral effects. That said, firm shares and numbers remain relevant since at least one default measure of substitution (the "diversion ratio") relies precisely on the market shares of important rivals in a market.[57] In addition, the FTC has explained that in unilateral effects analysis, significant competitors "usually have market shares in excess of 10%."[58] As a result, while the concentration standards and the weakening degree of enforcement of those standards are issues central to the competitive problem of coordination, they remain relevant to the concern over unilateral effects.

What is clear from this analysis is the effect of this weakening of merger enforcement over the past twenty-five years. That effect is, of course, to have permitted an entire range of mergers that were previously challenged with substantial frequency. Aggregate data confirming this was presented in Chapter 2. Here we note, anecdotally, countless mergers that have transformed airlines, brewing, finance, industrial chemicals, eyeglasses, drug stores, supermarkets, cable TV, hospitals, dog food, waste management, dialysis centers, veterinary clinics, pharmaceutical companies, pharmacy benefits managers, seed companies, meat processing, casket manufacture, washing machine manufacturing, diapers, and car rentals, among countless others. These mergers have in turn directly affected the strength of competition in markets throughout the economy.

The very first—and a threshold—step for strengthening merger control should be for the agencies to begin enforcing their own written standards. These are, after all, stated policy, well founded in economics, largely accepted by the courts, and requiring nothing more than agency determination to act accordingly.

---

56 Malcolm Coate, *The Merger Review Process at the Federal Trade Commission from 1989 to 2016* (February 28, 2018), SSRN: https://ssrn.com/abstract=2955987.

57 See, for example, discussion in Carl Shapiro, *Mergers with Differentiated Products*, 10 Antitrust, 23-30 (Spring 1996).

58 FTC, Horizontal Merger Investigations Data, Washington DC, 2013.

RECOMMENDATIONS:[59]

> *(1) The FTC and DOJ must commit to enforcing the market share and concentration standards in the Merger Guidelines as written.*
>
> *(2) The agencies need to make clear that the mergers falling near the thresholds are not in fact subject to significantly looser standards than written, but rather will receive the full degree of scrutiny that the relevant thresholds imply.*

4.2 The Structural Presumption

As was discussed in Chapter 3, both the numerical thresholds for concentration and shares in the Merger Guidelines as well as the significance attached to them for particular mergers have varied over time. The original 1968 standards were both stringent and clear. They said that in concentrated markets, the Justice Department "will ordinarily challenge mergers between firms accounting for" the various stated market shares. The term "ordinarily" was widely interpreted as effectively a presumption against such mergers, and the actual practice of the Justice Department did nothing to dispel that view.

This doctrine—the so-called "structural presumption" —had unimpeachable underpinnings. It originated with the Supreme Court's 1963 opinion in the *Philadelphia National Bank* case.[60] There the court articulated the proposition that sizeable mergers in highly concentrated markets were so inherently likely to be anticompetitive that no full-blown inquiry into their particular effects was necessary. Rather, the antitrust agencies could simply ascertain that there were no decisive offsetting considerations, and then prohibit the merger. The basis for this presumption was said to be convincing economic evidence about the competitive harms from such mergers.

Each version of the Merger Guidelines has had language seeking to convey the importance to be attached to market structure and, by implication, the degree to which mergers with high market shares and high concentration might be subject to a true presumption. The language has varied in ways that conveyed different—and declining—likelihoods of agency challenge in actual practice, that is, a weakening of the presumption. The first revision of the Guidelines, in 1982, omitted the declaration that such mergers would "ordinarily" be challenged, replacing it with the statement that such

---

59 These and all subsequent recommendations in this book are compiled in Appendix A.

60 *U.S. v. Philadelphia National Bank*, 374 U.S. 321 (1963).

mergers were "likely to create or enhance market power." The 2010 revision of the Guidelines added a further twist on the language by combining the qualifiers "presumed" and "likely" into the statement that such mergers would be "presumed to be likely" to increase market power.

Combined with the decline in the numerical enforcement standards, this weakening of the structural presumption has resulted in ever fewer mergers even of very large size simply being prohibited as inherently or obviously anticompetitive. Instead, the agencies now routinely undertake full-blown analyses of even the largest mergers for their specific anticompetitive potential—not only calculating shares and concentration, but evaluating all possibly offsetting factors, including claimed benefits from the merger, and developing a theory of how each merger is likely to result in competitive harm.[61]

To the extent that the necessary information is available and determinative, this approach may well be ideal, but in practice it imposes substantial requirements on the agencies. It requires an understanding of the firms' business models, their likely strategic use of assets post-merger, specific anticompetitive opportunities created by the merger, and so forth. It also increasingly draws in high-powered economic consultants on both sides, vigorously debating data, statistical models, econometric estimates, etc. to the dismay, but not necessarily the enlightenment, of the judiciary. It was precisely for these reasons that the presumption was devised. It brings collective understanding to a specific case. As such, it can be both a sufficient and an efficient alternative to the expansive, expensive, and often ambiguous alternative approach. [62]

Why, then, has the structural presumption played such a diminished role in merger enforcement? One reason is the natural preference for direct evidence of likely competitive harm in the form, for example, of business strategy documents detailing planned price increases, or for economic evidence corroborating an accepted model of anticompetitive firm behavior. Perhaps more importantly, however, the structural presumption has fallen victim to the claim that it would make too many Type I errors—challenging mergers that are in fact competitively benign or beneficial. This argument has gained support in the courts and elsewhere despite the lack of any sys-

---

61 While some would debate any example, prospective mergers such as that proposed in 2014 between U.S. Foods and Sysco would seem transparently anticompetitive, but nonetheless involved a protracted inquiry at the Federal Trade Commission.

62 These considerations have prompted Posner to describe open-ended inquiries as a "blot on the judiciary" and to endorse the use of presumptions. Richard Posner & C. Scott Hemphill, *Philadelphia National Bank at 50: An Interview with Richard Posner*, 80 ANTITRUST LAW JOURNAL, 205-218 (2015).

tematic evidence in support of it, and without equal attention to the costs of errors of omission—that is, overlooking anticompetitive mergers.[63] Nonetheless, these arguments have largely prevailed and added to the agencies' reluctance to advance such arguments in court. The result has been a lesser role for the structural presumption in the Merger Guidelines than the Supreme Court itself endorsed.

It should be noted that merger control policy is an exercise in prediction. It involves choosing a method for forecasting the effects of a proposed merger that in all likelihood differs from any other merger previously seen. As such, it requires accepting some nonzero probability of prediction error. These facts have led some to propose an "error cost" framework for assessing antitrust actions. In this framework the costs of Type I errors, the costs of Type II errors, plus the administrative costs of the antitrust process should be minimized.

Baker has criticized use of this framework by Chicago school scholars to justify inaction with respect to various competitive concerns, not just mergers.[64] He documents the general falsity of the assumptions that entry is generally easy, that oligopolies and cartels are unstable and fall of their own accord, and that monopolies innovate more—all critical to the view that mergers and concentration should be of minimal concern.

Salop has recently developed a more rigorous framework along these lines based on decision theory, the *ex ante* probabilities, and the probative value of evidence. Crucially, he has noted that the evidence available or revealed even in a detailed analytical process is unlikely to be dispositive.[65] This will result in residual uncertainty with respect to the Type I and Type II errors, the economic costs of each of those errors, and the administrative costs of a

---

63 A notable illustration of this view—albeit not from a merger case—is the Supreme Court's decision in the *Trinko* case, which opined as follows: "Against the slight benefits of antitrust intervention here, we must weigh a realistic assessment of its costs....Mistaken inferences and the resulting false condemnations 'are especially costly, because they chill the very conduct the antitrust laws are designed to protect...' The cost of false positives counsels against an undue expansion of Section 2 liability." *Verizon Comm. v. Law Offices of Curtis Trinko*, 540 US 398, 414 (2004), quoting from the court's earlier *Matshushita* decision. No actual rate or costs of false positives were cited in the opinion; rather, they were simply stated to be "realistic." *Matsushita Electric Industrial Co. v. Zenith Radio Corp.*, 475 U.S.574 (1986).

64 Jon Baker, *Taking the Error Out of 'Error Cost' Analysis: What's Wrong With Antitrust's Right*, 80 ANTITRUST LAW JOURNAL (2015).

65 Steven Salop, *The Evolution and Vitality of Merger Presumptions: A Decision-Theoretic Approach*, 80 ANTITRUST LAW JOURNAL (2015).

case-specific inquiry. These considerations should affect the policy choice. To illustrate, suppose that all or almost all mergers with certain observable characteristics (e.g., mergers to monopoly) are anticompetitive. In that case, a blanket policy—a presumption—against such mergers likely represents an effective approach since it would make few if any errors. In addition, it would require minimal resources relative to a full-blown analysis of each such merger. But critically, there is no guarantee that a full-blown inquiry "gets it right" anyway, despite the expenditure of considerable resources in the process. As a result, a strong—perhaps even irrebuttable—presumption might represent optimal policy toward mergers to monopoly. Even if that rule were to make the very occasional error, it would be very small and likely no greater than the error rate from a full-blown and costly case-specific analysis.

By extension, an analogous argument might be made with respect to mergers to duopoly ("3-to-2 mergers"). Even if a presumption against such mergers might result in a slightly greater error rate, it might still be optimal policy. And if that were to be the case, the same question could be asked about 4-to-3 mergers, and so forth, until the balance of errors and costs no longer favored a presumption. This example underscores the crucial nature of the error rate (as well as associated costs) in coming to a determination about the value of a presumption based on market structure. And to complete the story, mergers with characteristics that all or nearly all of the time are associated with benign outcomes could be addressed by an analogous presumption in their favor.[66]

Recent statistical analysis has cast some light on the underlying issues and factors. My own work in this area has addressed the magnitude of Type I error from a structural presumption by calculating the actual error rate that would have arisen if a structural presumption had in fact been used on a group of past mergers whose actual outcomes are known.[67] For these purposes, the actual outcomes are determined from careful studies of the effects of actual consummated mergers on prices.[68] I have compiled all of the existing qualifying studies, arrayed the mergers by the level of concentration in the affected markets, and then determined what fraction of mergers "above the line" —that is, with concentration in excess of some hypothetical standard or presumption—in fact turned out to result in price increases. The

---

66 Contrast, for example, Douglas Ginsburg & Joshua Wright, *Philadelphia National Bank: Bad Economics, Bad Law, Good Riddance*, 80 ANTITRUST LAW JOURNAL 2 (2015).

67 John Kwoka, *The Structural Presumption and Safe Harbor in Merger Review: False Positives or Unwarranted Concerns?* 82 ANTITRUST LAW JOURNAL 1, (2017).

68 The actual technique is usually termed a "merger retrospective." These will be discussed more fully in Chapter 7.

higher that fraction, the stronger the basis for a presumption; the smaller the fraction, the greater the support for concern that a presumption would too often erroneously attack benign or beneficial mergers.

The results of this research are reported in Table 4.2. Not surprisingly, it shows that the tighter the standard, the lower the error rate. More concretely, use of the current Merger Guidelines thresholds for a presumption of likely market power—an HHI in excess of 2500 with a change of at least 200—correctly predicts the actual empirically tested outcome in 86 percent of cases. That is, the greatly feared Type I error is no more than 14 percent, and this is, of course, a presumption rather than an irrebuttable or conclusive determination. A stricter standard—that is, with a larger HHI—increases the percent of merger outcomes correctly predicted.

Even more striking are the results from using as an alternative measure of concentration the number of significant competitors that remain after a merger. Since a "significant competitor" is a firm that is large enough to influence the strength of competition and the resulting market equilibrium, this measure reflects both the level and change in HHI. As shown in Table 4.3, in this dataset, all mergers with five or fewer remaining competitors were found to be anticompetitive. Even a criterion of six or fewer has an error rate of only 5.3 percent.

TABLE 4.2

Predictive Power of Merger Guidelines Criteria: HHI and Change > 200

HHI	Number of mergers exceeding threshold	Number anticompetitive	Number procompetitive	Percent Correct
4000	10	9	1	90
3500	14	13	1	92.9
3000	17	15	2	88.2
2500	21	18	3	85.7
2000	24	21	3	87.5

TABLE 4.3

Predictive Power of Number of Competitors

Incremental Significant Competitor	Anti	Pro	Percent Correct
1	1	0	100
2	2	0	100
3			
4	4	0	100
5	7	0	100
6	4	1	80
7	2	2	50
8	1	2	33.3

While the number of mergers analyzed in this study is not overly large, this evidence—which is the best available—strongly suggests that reliance on structural criteria against certain mergers is well founded. A presumption based on HHI and its change, or on the number of remaining significant competitors, would make relatively few errors. Moreover, given the costs of conducting a full analysis of each case and the uncertainty of the gain in resulting accuracy, the advantages of a structure-based presumption against certain mergers are all the stronger.

It might also be noted that this same research raises questions about the other structure-based presumption in the guidelines commonly known as the "safe harbor." This provision states that "[m]ergers resulting in unconcentrated markets [HHI less than 1500] are unlikely to have adverse competitive effects and ordinarily require no further analysis." The safe harbor has received virtually no critical review and has been subject to no testing, but my evidence shows that a considerable number of anticompetitive mergers fall below that concentration threshold. By the same criteria as above, the frequency of these harmful mergers is an indication that the application of this lower structural presumption for the purpose of automatically clearing mergers has in fact erroneously approved anticompetitive mergers. This is the Type II error that has received much less attention in merger review.

Interestingly, while the agencies tend to avoid reliance on the structural presumption in merger review and judicial proceedings, they routinely use it in their own policy analysis. This is evident from agency explanations for the remedies they devise for specific mergers. For example, the FTC's explanation of its settlement of the recent merger of the Ahold and Delhaize supermarket chains includes the following straightforward explanation for divestitures it required in 46 geographic markets:

> Under the 2010 Department of Justice and Federal Trade Commission Horizontal Merger Guidelines, an acquisition that results in an HHI in excess of 2500 and increases HHI by more than 200 significantly increases concentration in a highly concentrated market and therefore is presumed anticompetitive. With the exception of one market [footnote omitted], each of the relevant geographic markets identified above meets the ... presumption.[69]

This declaration is followed by an enumeration of markets where the merger would be two-to-one, three-to-two, four-to-three and so forth, down to one market where the merger would be seven-to-six. Divestitures were ordered in every single one of those cases based simply on a count of competitors.

In short, the available evidence, analytics, and even some agency practices establish that there should be an important role for a strong presumption against mergers with certain, specifiable structural characteristics. There is in fact good evidence to support a stronger presumption than the standard now stated in the Merger Guidelines. The presumption should be all-but-irrebuttable, allowing only for counter-arguments that are "indisputable and decisive."[70]

RECOMMENDATIONS:

> *(1) The agencies need to explicitly endorse the doctrine of a structural presumption. They should use that doctrine to prohibit large mergers in high concentration industries without further analysis, subject only to sharply limited counter-arguments from merging parties.*

---

69 FTC, Analysis of Agreement Containing Consent Order to Aid Public Comment, *In the Matter of Koninklijke Ahold N.V. and Delhaise Group NV/SA*, File No. 151-0175, 2019. For other examples of explicit reliance on structural criteria, see the FTC consent orders and accompanying analyses for the merger of Fresenius Medical Care AG and Liberty Dialysis Holdings in 2012, and for that of Teva Pharmaceuticals and Allergan in 2017.

70 One recent step towards re-establishing a true presumption is contained in legislation introduced into Congress in 2017. That bill—the Consolidation Prevention and Competition Promotion Act of 2017—would place the burden on certain "mega-mergers" to show that they would not diminish competition, reversing the current burden on the agencies to show competitive harm.

(2) The agencies should employ a nearly-irrebuttable presumption against mergers resulting in one, two, or three competitors, and a still formidable presumption against those resulting in four or five competitors. Explicit evidence of effects is not necessary.

(3) The agencies must revise their declaration that mergers below some threshold generally raise no competitive concerns and ordinarily will not be challenged.

(4) The agencies should undertake further statistical analysis of the relevant share and concentration thresholds.

4.3 Observations on Guidelines and Presumptions

This discussion of guidelines and presumptions for merger enforcement has highlighted their value to the business and legal communities as well as to the agencies themselves. For all their imperfections, the Horizontal Merger Guidelines do provide insight into the agencies' thinking, so that parties contemplating mergers can better anticipate how those actions will be viewed. In addition, their explicit nature allows interested parties to evaluate and suggest improvements in the agencies' analytical framework. The use of presumptions similarly provides clarity and consistency to the business and legal communities regarding the policy response to mergers with particular characteristics. Presumptions relieve the agencies of the often substantial burden of building cases from the ground up against all mergers regardless of how obvious the competitive concerns may be, and striving to build cases where the precise anticompetitive conduct is difficult to predict and impossible to establish *ex ante.*

For these reasons, additional guidelines should be considered in other areas where the agencies' methodology could usefully be set forth. This would seem useful in at least two areas, both discussed in later chapters. One is vertical integration, where current economic thinking about possible competitive concerns is sufficiently concrete as to permit a statement providing guidance to outside parties. Indeed, the Justice Department and FTC have recently released draft guidelines for vertical mergers. A second area concerns the treatment of innovation. Here the economic framework may be more difficult to fully specify, but that should not prevent issuance of an outline of a structured approach that would set out screens and factors deserving consideration. One can also envision useful efforts to provide guidance with respect to other areas of antitrust concern.

The use of presumptions might be extended into other areas of antitrust policy where the frequency of procompetitive outcomes is not large and/or when the alternative case-specific inquiry is costly and not likely to significantly reduce the error rate. In these cases, a presumption can be an efficient as well as effective enforcement strategy. One area, which will be discussed further in Chapter 8, concerns mergers and acquisitions in the tech sector. Other candidate areas for possible presumptions might include efficiencies and entry conditions (as will be discussed below) and with respect to non-merger matters, strategically low prices ("predation"), tying and bundling, selective discounting, and certain distribution practices.

To be clear, the standard should not be perfect accuracy in predicting the outcome, nor even complete characterization of scenarios, but rather specification of criteria for challenges that are superior to full-blown, rule of reason inquiries for all cases, given the costs and uncertainties associated with the latter. Much as with the structural presumption, this device can make merger control more efficient as well as more effective.

RECOMMENDATIONS:

(1) *The agencies need to work towards issuing guidelines on topics such as vertical mergers and innovation in order to provide guidance and clarity about their analytical approach.*

(2) *The agencies should develop reliable presumptions wherever feasible and efficient relative to a case-by-case approach. These would be useful for addressing claims of merger-related efficiencies and ease of entry into markets.*

CHAPTER 5

RETHINKING "PLUS OR MINUS" FACTORS:
Efficiencies, Entry Conditions, and Potential Competition

About 1500 proposed mergers each year are of the size that triggers the legal requirement for filing preliminary information with the antitrust agencies. The previous chapter focused on criteria for initial screening and treatment of those mergers for possible anticompetitive outcomes. Based on these criteria and other factors, the agencies initiate formal investigations in about 3 percent of these proposed mergers. They issue so-called "second requests" for detailed information about these mergers, and then analyze the likely competitive effects of each. The analytical procedure set out in the Merger Guidelines specifies that the analysis should consider two factors that might offset an initial judgment disapproving a merger and two other considerations that might heighten concern with a merger. This chapter addresses all of these "plus factors" and "minus factors."

The possibly offsetting factors are the ease or difficulty of entry into the market, and the efficiencies that may derive from the merger. Easy entry can reverse an initial determination against a merger, and cost savings or other possible benefits may weigh significantly in its favor. This chapter begins by addressing both of these "minus" factors, contrasting economic understanding of the role and significance of entry and efficiencies with their actual role in merger analysis in recent years. As we shall see, analysis has become excessively receptive to these offsetting considerations, a policy stance that must be reversed.

This chapter next addresses two quite different mechanisms through which a merger can in fact raise competitive concerns that go beyond the simple price-elevation analysis described above. One such "plus" scenario is when a merger creates or enhances a barrier to entry by other firms or an impediment to growth by smaller firms in the market. The resulting effects on entry, growth, and dynamism were documented in an earlier chapter. The second concern is with mergers that eliminate a potential entrant that constrains the incumbent firm or firms, thereby permitting the latter to raise price without fear of triggering entry. As we shall see, while efficiencies and entry as defenses have received considerable deference, the latter arguments—new entry barriers and the elimination of potential competitors—have received much less so.

Our discussion begins with the two facts potentially offsetting opposition to a merger, and then shifts to the two competitive offenses. Each section concludes with specific recommendations for strengthening merger enforcement in each of these areas.

5.1 Efficiencies and Other Merger-Related Benefits

Economics has long recognized the importance of efficiencies from mergers, but their treatment in successive Merger Guidelines has grown more accommodating over time, reflecting agency practice. The 1982 Guidelines stated that some modest efficiencies were to be expected from mergers generally and that those were already reflected in the concentration thresholds defining competitively problematic mergers. Only in "extraordinary" circumstances, those guidelines said, would the agencies need to consider specific claims. This formulation was an effort to restrict the burden on the agencies by setting a high bar for case-specific claims. Under pressure from merger advocates, however, this was soon relaxed.

In 1992 the new Guidelines stated only that "in a majority of cases" the Guidelines thresholds should suffice for the realization of efficiencies, a statement leaving a substantially larger fraction than the residual from "extraordinary" circumstances. This encouraged many more case-specific claims, imposing greater burdens on the agencies and creating new opportunities for merging parties to dispute possible challenges. This basic policy statement was repeated in the 2010 Merger Guidelines, but those guidelines went one important step farther. With the introduction of the theory of unilateral effects and the associated concept of upward pricing pressure, efficiencies were fully integrated into the framework for analyzing mergers. Upward pricing pressure explicitly trades off anticompetitive price increases against measured cost savings, abandoning the more ambiguous treatment of efficiencies in earlier guidelines and, indeed, in contrast to court opinions that have generally rejected efficiencies as offsets to otherwise competitively problematic mergers.[71]

---

71 Upward pricing pressure assesses likely price effects by weighing the likely price increase against any cost savings. While a useful analytical tool, it has provided validation for treating efficiency claims as an integral component for analyzing mergers.

To be sure, the Merger Guidelines make clear that not all efficiency claims are to be credited to a merger. To be recognized as a potential offset, efficiencies must satisfy certain criteria: They must be verifiable rather than speculative. They must be merger-specific, that is, not achievable in some other, competitively benign way. And they must be passed on at least in part to consumers. Nonetheless, this evolution of treatment in the Merger Guidelines has resulted in claims of efficiencies being transformed from being exceptional to becoming the norm. And there is little doubt that these claims matter. Agency discussion of any number of mergers makes clear that they can play a significant role in the final determination of a merger's competitive effects.[72] Economic evidence and practical considerations, however, suggest that such claims should be dismissed more often, more fully, and sooner.

The key economic factor is simply the wealth of evidence that mergers generally do not produce significant efficiencies. Previously cited work by Blonigen & Pierce searched for statistical evidence of efficiency gains generally in manufacturing plants that were involved in mergers between 1997 and 2007. They found "little evidence for plant- or firm-level productivity effects from M&A activity on average, nor for other efficiency gains often cited as possible from M&A activity, including reallocation of activity across plants or scale efficiencies in non-productive units of the firm."[73] A meta-analysis of retrospective studies examining the effects of mergers on cost savings arrived at much the same conclusion. It found that those savings averaged less than 1 percent.[74] The business literature concurs. A McKinsey study compared the actual cost synergies achieved by merging firms against pre-merger claims, and concluded that "most buyers routinely overvalue the synergies to be had from acquisitions."[75] In about a quarter of the cases the overestimate exceeded 25 percent.

More detailed evidence at the sectoral and case study level is consistent. A recent study of numerous hospital mergers confirms marginal cost

---

72 As one of many examples, at the end of its investigation of the merger of Delta and Northwest Airlines, the Justice Department issued a press release citing "efficiencies such as cost savings in airport operations, information technology, supply chain economics, and fleet optimization... [as well as consumer] benefit from improved service made possible by combining under single ownership the complementary aspects of the airlines' networks" as the basis for approval despite competitive overlaps on some routes.

73 Blonigen & Pierce, op. cit.

74 John Kwoka & Shawn Kilpatrick, *Nonprice Effects of Mergers*, 63 ANTITRUST BULLETIN 2, 169-182 (2018).

75 Scott A. Christofferson, Robert S. McNish & Diane L. Sias, *Where Mergers Go Wrong*, MCKINSEY QUARTERLY, 1–6, (2004).

reductions of only about 1.5 percent.[76]   A study of airline mergers by the American Antitrust Institute found that airlines routinely underestimated system integration costs, sometimes by as much as 200 percent.[77]   The DOJ and FCC analysis of benefits from AT&T's proposed acquisition of T-Mobile was shown to rely on erroneous assumptions about technology deployment.[78] Somewhat farther back in time was the FTC's analysis of the proposed merger of Staples and Office Depot.   Whereas the parties claimed cost savings of 7.2 percent, the agency found plausible only 1.4 percent.[79]

While as always more evidence is needed, there is no current basis for the belief that mergers generally result in substantial cost savings, notwithstanding the frequency of claims to the contrary. This is not to dispute that sizeable efficiencies may arise in some small fraction of cases.   But in assuming the burden of determining whether virtually every merger is that exceptional case, the agencies must evaluate most such claims, even in order to dispute or dismiss them.   Moreover, while the agencies' evaluations exclude many specious claims, post-merger evidence indicates that other claims do in fact survive. This is not surprising since in evaluating efficiency claims, the agencies operate at a significant informational disadvantage relative to the merging parties. The parties know their technology and input costs—both current and expected—better than does the antitrust agency. In addition, there is at present no downside to the parties for offering even speculative claims about efficiencies in the hope that at least some will survive agency review (although, as shall be seen, that can be remedied). The result of this asymmetry is that claims that cannot be disproved often receive at least some credit in the agencies' analysis.

Over time, the burden on the reviewing agencies has further increased due to changes in the nature of "efficiency" claims. The 1992 Guidelines directed attention to cost savings due to "economies of scale, better integration of production facilities, plant specialization, lower transportation

---

76 Stuart Craig, Matthew Grennan & Ashley Swanson, *Mergers and Marginal Costs: New Evidence on Hospital Buyer Power* (NBER Working Paper No. 24926, August 2018).

77 Diana Moss, *Delivering the Benefits? Efficiencies and Airline Mergers*, AMERICAN ANTITRUST INSTITUTE, (November 21, 2013), SSRN: https://ssrn.com/abstract=2547673.

78 Patrick DeGraba & Gregory Rosston, *The Proposed Merger of AT&T and T-Mobile*, in THE ANTITRUST REVOLUTION, (J. Kwoka & L. White, eds., 7th edition, 2019).

79 Serdar Dalkir & Frederick Warren-Boulton, *Prices, Market Definition, and the Effects of Merger: Staples-Office Depot*, in THE ANTITRUST REVOLUTION, op. cit.

costs, and similar efficiencies relating to specific manufacturing, servicing, or distribution operations."[80] These are traditional efficiencies—those associated with size, or scope, or integration—but as the agencies have become more skilled in evaluating (and often rejecting) such claims, firms increasingly have asserted other types of efficiencies and non-efficiency benefits from merging.[81] These newer merger-related benefits[82] include quality improvements, investment incentives, network economies, and efficiencies from vertical integration. One common feature of these claimed merger benefits is that they are considerably more difficult to assess and quantify than traditional cost savings.

Examples of these include the following:

- **Quality Improvements.** Rather than shifting the cost curve, better quality products or services would shift the demand curve upward, arguably signaling consumer benefits. But estimating a shift in a demand curve due to a quality improvement, and then evaluating the resulting consumer surplus gain is a much more challenging task than measuring a reduction in variable costs.

- **Greater Investment.** A frequent claim of merging parties is that larger size results in greater returns and hence strengthens their incentive to invest. But it is at least as likely that size blunts their incentives as firms acquire market power and diminished need to pursue new initiatives. In any event, claims of greater investment incentives are very difficult to evaluate since investment decisions are highly variable, multidimensional, and longer term in nature.

- **Network Economies.** Network effects are consumer benefits arising from aggregating ever more users to the same service, most obviously on communications platforms but also for certain hardware-software combinations and other products. Network effects can be difficult to quantify but should not be accepted uncritically for that reason.

---

80 U.S. Dep't of Justice and FTC. 1992. Horizontal Merger Guidelines.

81 The AAI study of airlines reported that in four mergers between 2005 and 2012, the percent of all claimed efficiencies consisting of network effects rose from 45 to 70 percent, 70-80 percent, and finally over 80 percent, in that order.

82 It is not entirely accurate to call quality, investment, network and vertical effects "efficiencies." but they continue to be described as such. A better term would be "synergies." For further discussion, see John Kwoka, *The Changing Nature of Efficiencies in Mergers and Merger Analysis*, 60 ANTITRUST BULLETIN 3, 231-249, (2015).

• **Vertical Economies.** For mergers that also have vertical dimensions, parties routinely claim credit for such factors as avoidance of double marginalization and more subtle cost savings from integration. As will be discussed below, true vertical economies are often claimed but much less often proven.

As noted, these various merger-related "benefits" have been playing increasingly important—and often controversial—roles in recent cases. In the *Ticketmaster-Live Nation* merger, for example, the parties asserted there would be efficiencies from transactions costs savings and from the avoidance of double marginalization.[83] In airline mergers and code-sharing agreements, the parties have routinely asserted substantial dollar benefits—often in the hundreds of millions of dollars—to consumers from creating more single-carrier routes and more frequent service on any single route.[84] And in the recent *AT&T-Time Warner* case, the Justice Department broke precedent and conceded that the vertical merger would save more than $300 million by eliminating double marginalization, despite doubts about its magnitude and importance. More generally, the already-cited McKinsey study reported that 70 percent of their surveyed mergers failed to achieve their expected "revenue-synergies."[85]

In short, the importance attributed to efficiencies in merger review would seem to exceed their role in actual business practice. Rather, the balance of error types and costs, together with administrative costs would seem to make efficiency claims a good candidate for a strong contrary presumption. That is, with relatively few credible efficiency claims, with significant competitive harms from allowing otherwise anticompetitive mergers, with substantial resource costs for evaluating claims, and with only partial correction from such evaluations, a strong presumption against efficiency claims would seem justified. A presumption would accommodate true and substantial efficiencies without encumbering the review process with numerous modest and doubtful claims.

---

83 See John Kwoka, "Rockonomics: The Ticketmaster-Live Nation Merger and the Rock Concert Business," in THE ANTITRUST REVOLUTION (J. Kwoka & L. White, eds., 7th ed. 2019). The term double marginalization refers to a setting where an upstream company with market power charges a markup to the downstream firm which in turn marks up the markup. The issues involved here will be discussed below in the context of vertical mergers.

84 See Israel, et al., op. cit. Even if correct, it might be noted that these benefits may not accrue to the same consumers that are arguably harmed by reduced competition on certain routes.

85 McKinsey, op. cit.

Various policy reforms with respect to efficiencies and other benefits are therefore necessary in order to rebalance the current overly receptive posture of the agencies toward such claims. These include, most obviously, tightening the standards, but also requiring *ex post* review in order to determine whether the promised offsets in fact occurred. If not, the agencies should revisit any merger whose approval was contingent on the claimed efficiencies, and be prepared to take action against the merger even if consummated. This posture would have the desirable effect of deterring dubious *ex ante* claims of efficiencies by the merging parties, which now suffer no adverse consequences from any such claims.

RECOMMENDATIONS:

(1) The guidelines must clearly state that the share and concentration thresholds allow for standard or typical efficiencies and benefits so that only the most unusual or exceptional or extraordinary claims will be considered on a case-by-case basis. Consideration should be given to setting some minimum efficiency for case-specific analysis.

(2) The guidelines need to make clear that even such extraordinary claims must be verified by evidence from past practice or from documentation prepared in the ordinary course of business well before the merger proposal. This would give little or no weight to claims and reports about prospective efficiencies that have been prepared only for the purpose of a merger submission to the agencies.

(3) The guidelines should make clear that extraordinary claims of efficiencies will be subject to ex post review by the agency. Where the full extent of claimed efficiencies within a two- or three-year period cannot be verified with clear and convincing evidence, the merger itself will be subject to remedial action by the agency.

5.2 Ease of Entry as a Defense

The importance of entry conditions in principle is not in dispute, of course, but what has been in dispute is the degree to which ease of entry actually disciplines incumbent firms and whether the prospect of entry is an adequate substitute for policy action. On the one hand, without evidence, the Chicago school argued that markets are generally "self-correcting," arguing that excessively profitable incumbents would necessarily attract entrants that would dissipate such profits and the dominance that fostered them. An extreme version of this theory—known as "contestability"—concluded that with perfectly easy entry and exit, even an incumbent monopoly raised no competitive concern because it would lack the ability to profitably raise price. If it attempted to raise price, entrants would quickly and costlessly enter and undercut its price, even displacing the incumbent. On the other hand, actual markets often seem resistant to entry even when profit signals are clear. Indeed, the very market pointed to by advocates as illustrating extreme ease of entry—airlines—fails the test of "contestability." Empirical studies have emphatically rejected this to be the case in airlines, or for that matter any other industry.[86]

With actual entry subject to practical considerations, successive Merger Guidelines have sought to specify the criteria for entry conditions that would represent effective constraints on market power for merging firms. The current 2010 Guidelines state simply that a "merger is not likely to enhance market power if entry into the market is so easy that the merged firm and its remaining rivals in the market...could not profitably raise price or otherwise reduce competition." Those guidelines go on to note that such entry must be sufficiently fast (within two years), sufficiently certain (profitable to the entrant), and sufficiently sizeable (capable of reversing the competitive harms).

While these criteria would seem to represent economically sensible screens against implausible, inadequate, or untimely entry, in fact the agencies have too often accepted what seem to be unlikely or even implausible arguments about the possibility of entry.[87] This excess deference to claims that entry is easy and sufficient to allow mergers is evident in the previously cited FTC data on its enforcement actions between 1996 and 2011. For that period, the FTC evaluated a total of 45 mergers where the agency judged entry to be "easy." None of these mergers triggered any further enforcement action—not one, not even the four mergers where HHI exceeded 5000 (denoting a duopoly) and HHI rose by more than 2500 (two very large firms).

Clearly, persuading the agency that entry is "easy" has been tantamount to gaining approval of a merger regardless of the level of concentration or the size of the merging firms. Compounding this, some courts have also treated evidence of entry as a trump card rescuing otherwise anticom-

---

86 Among many studies, see for example, John Kwoka, Phillippe Alepin & Kevin Hearle, *From the Fringe to the Forefront: Low-Cost Carriers and Airline Price Determination*, 48 REVIEW OF INDUSTRIAL ORGANIZATION 3, (2016).

87 More worrisome yet are some agency efforts to virtually create entrants where none exist. In proposed mergers of U.S. Foods and Sysco, in Office Depot and Staples, and most recently Sprint and T-Mobile, the need to replace a competitor lost as a result of the merger has prompted efforts by the agencies to bolster or construct an effective new competitor. This issue will be discussed further in the context of merger remedies.

petitive mergers. The court decisions in the *Baker Hughes* merger and in *Syufy* overturned agency challenges by courts that concluded, on slender evidence, that entry was sufficiently easy to negate competitive harm from these mergers.[88] This excessive deference paid to the possibility and effectiveness of entry needs to be revised to be more in accordance with current economic understanding and evidence.

Given this potency of the entry argument, the agencies are routinely confronted with merging parties' arguments that entry is quite easy and that they therefore need not be concerned with a particular merger. This grossly exaggerates the generality and adequacy of entry as a solution to a concern with a merger. We note that the earlier evidence about declining rates of entry and numbers of firms in the economy as a whole signals a sharp reduction in the overall pool of firms capable and poised to enter various markets. In a vast array of other industries, impediments to entry are the norm, not the exception. Types of strategies that handicap rivals or exclude potential competitors include raising rivals' costs of operation, practices that limit competitors' access to distribution channels, refusals to deal with or supply rivals, strategic discounting or tying that locks customers into incumbent suppliers, vertical integration that forecloses or handicaps rivals, standards setting that disadvantages potential rivals, creating obstacles to interoperability, and manipulation of the regulatory process, among others.[89]

More specific examples are well documented. As previously noted, a large brewer may be able to force a distributor into some exclusionary practice that handicaps smaller brewers by threatening to withhold its own high-volume, "must-have" product.[90] Similarly, an important food manufacturer may be able to secure more advantageous shelf space arrangements with a supermarket, handicapping new entrants and smaller firms. A large airline may control gates or landing rights, or be able to engage in strategic pricing across routes.[91] Or a sufficiently large firm may be able to pressure other firms to deal only, or on more advantageous terms, with itself, thereby cut-

---

88 *United States v. Baker Hughes, Inc.*, 908 F.2d 981 (D.C. Cir. 1990); *United States v. Syufy Enterprises*, 903 F.2d 659 (9th Cir. 1990). See also Jonathan Baker, *The Problem with Baker Hughes and Syufy: On the Role of Entry in Merger Analysis*, ANTITRUST LAW JOURNAL, (1997).

89 For a longer list and extensive discussion, see Jonathan Baker, *Exclusion as a Core Competition Concern*, 88 ANTITRUST LAW JOURNAL 527-589(2013).

90 See Chapter 2 for this and other examples.

91 See, for example, Federico Ciliberto & Jonathan Williams, "Limited Access to Airport Facilities and Market Power in the Airline Indusry," Journal of Law and Economics, August 2010.

ting out independent single-stage rivals. Or an integrated firm may simply foreclose those rivals from either necessary inputs or customers it controls, thereby handicapping those rivals to the benefit of its own businesses.[92]

Many of these impediments are subtle. Some have alternative explanations that are difficult to assess, much less refute. Few produce immediate anticompetitive effects. Rather, their effects are indirect and delayed, and may only erode rather than fully prevent competition. But they all can help insulate incumbents from the constraining effect of a possible entrant and from actual future entry that would undermine the incumbent's position. As a result, claims of easy entry must be reviewed ever more skeptically in order to avoid unleashing anticompetitive mergers on markets that are vulnerable to market power.

RECOMMENDATIONS:

(1) *The agencies must treat claims of easy entry extremely cautiously since an erroneously accepted claim can undermine a determination of anticompetitive effects and lead to a lasting increase in market power.*

(2) *In evaluating claims of easy entry, more weight should be put on evidence of past entry and on business considerations favoring future entry than on conceptual arguments about the possibility of entry. If the market shows little sign of past entry, that should be taken as indicative of significant impediments to entry.*

5.3 Increased Entry Barriers as an Offense

Beyond this concern over the facile acceptance of the argument that entry is easy, there is another concern with entry conditions in the case of mergers. More or less the opposite of the above, this concern is that some mergers may actually create or enhance barriers to new entry or competition by existing rivals in the market. That is, by increasing a firm's size or structure, a merger may enhance its incentive or its ability to engage in such strategies. Indeed, all of the size-related barriers to entry and strategies to deter entry described above may be made possible by a merger.

Thus, simply by increasing its size, a merger of brewers may create sufficient additional leverage to impose restrictions on its distributors not to handle a rival's product. Similarly, a merger between food manufacturers

---

92 Further discussion of these strategies built on vertical integration appears below.

may help secure shelf space allocations that disadvantage smaller rivals. Indeed, any merger that gives a firm greater dominance and bargaining power makes a take-it-or-leave-it offer to a supplier or distributor more likely to be accepted—out of necessity—and the impediment to potential entrants and smaller rivals that much more substantial.

Another prominent example would arise if a large or dominant firm were to merge with an upstream supplier or downstream distributor. The resulting vertically integrated firm would be present in two markets and more insulated from entry to the extent that a possible entrant would need to enter at both stages of production, rather than just the one it previously targeted. Indeed, to the extent that the second market is unfamiliar to the possible entrant, the effective two-market barrier might represent a nearly prohibitive obstacle.[93]

The current Horizontal Merger Guidelines do not specifically mention as a competitive concern the possibility that a merger creates or enhances entry barriers. The only seemingly relevant reference is a statement that appears in a longer discussion of coordination and unilateral effects that reads in its entirety as follows: "Enhanced market power may also make it more likely that the merged entity can profitably and effectively engage in exclusionary conduct." There is no discussion of what the term "exclusionary conduct" encompasses, and no discussion as to how such conduct is to be analyzed or integrated into the broader analysis of the possible anticompetitive effects of a merger.

Baker has offered one of the few systematic analyses of exclusionary behavior.[94] He has documented various types of exclusion and their legal treatment and observed that the antitrust courts may be moving toward a "structured rule of reason" approach with respect to conduct that excludes. This would initially screen out unlikely cases based on structural conditions and then undertake a full analysis only on the remainder. This framework would shift policy in the right direction, but it would still not provide much guidance with respect to the defining characteristics of a merger that would significantly impede entry or growth of competition. As a result, it would not relieve the agency of the burden of a full analysis proving to the satisfaction of a court that a specific practice would (indeed, with high probability, will) do so.

This burden is considerably greater than with respect to concerns over coordinated effects or unilateral effects since greater obstacles to entry

---

93 This "two-market entry" problem will be discussed further below.

94 Jonathan Baker, "Exclusion as a Core Competitive Concern," ANTITRUST LAW JOURNAL, 2013.

are not likely to manifest themselves as price increases in any short or medium term. Rather, they work to insulate incumbent firms from longer-term entry, thereby conferring advantages on those incumbents as demand and other market conditions change to their benefit. Reforms here are necessary to re-establish the full force of the guidelines with respect to mergers that create or enhance such obstacles.

RECOMMENDATIONS:

> *(1) The Merger Guidelines need to describe more fully the competitive concerns with mergers that create or enhance entry barriers. The discussion should explain the various mechanisms, the specific competitive concerns, and the analytical approaches to their evaluation by the agencies, similar to their description of concerns with and analysis of price enhancement.*

> *(2) The basic framework for analyzing mergers must not be limited to likely price effects, but rather should define as competitively problematic any merger that materially impedes present or future competition by handicapping or preventing entry, growth, and stronger competition from an actual or potential rival.*

5.4 Eliminating Potential Entrants or Nascent Competitors

The Merger Guidelines direct attention to a small group of sellers of a product that can raise its price and make that price rise stick. This focus has left largely unaddressed the case of mergers that eliminate firms that threaten to enter the market, firms whose threatening presence may have constrained the incumbents and therefore whose elimination would relax that constraint and likely result in higher pricing by those incumbents. The relative lack of policy attention to mergers between an incumbent and a so-called "potential competitor" has resulted in increasingly common approval of such mergers without much notice, much less close scrutiny. But acquisitions of these potential entrants thwart the market's natural incentives to draw competitors into dominated markets, with longer term anticompetitive effects. A policy that has tended toward approval of these mergers needs to be reversed in order to prevent mergers that, by eliminating potential competitors, have reduced competition and harmed consumers.

There is no doubt in economics or logic that to the extent that an incumbent firm alters its pricing or other strategy out of concern for possible entry, the elimination of that threat causes competitive harm analogous to the harm from a merger that eliminates direct competition between actual incumbents. Furthermore, even if the incumbent were not aware that the outside firm was contemplating entry, such a merger might still be anticompetitive for a different reason. That reason is that such a merger eliminates the *actual* likelihood of future entry, entry that would deconcentrate and bring new competition to the market. In that case, while there would be no evidence of a pre-entry recognition by the incumbent firm that the outside firm was considering entry, it would still cause harm by sabotaging future competition.[95]

There is ample economic evidence that mergers eliminating potential competitors cause competitive harms similar to mergers between incumbents. Some of the most direct evidence involves the airline industry, where potential competition issues arise where a route is served by one of the merging carriers and the other is positioned to enter by virtue of serving one or both endpoints of the route.[96] Using standard data and methodology, Kwoka & Shumilkina find that the elimination of the potential entrant onto a route by merger with the incumbent results in a statistically significant price increase in the range of 5 to 6 percent.[97] This is about half the size of the price increase on "overlap" routes for the same merging carriers, that is, where both carriers are incumbents and the merger eliminates actual competition. Le uses the same methodology to examine a different airline merger and finds a similar—but larger—price effect from the elimination of both actual and potential competition.[98] These studies directly test the economic proposition that underlies the doctrine of potential competition and confirm its importance in the case of airlines.

Recent work by Cunningham et al. has added evidence of anticompetitive effects from acquisitions in a different industry. That study exam-

---

95 The first scenario is sometimes called a "perceived potential competitor," while the second is a "actual potential competitor." See John Kwoka, *Non-Incumbent Competition: Mergers Involving Constraining and Prospective Competitors*, CASE WESTERN RESERVE LAW REVIEW, (2001).

96 This is a fairly standard definition of potential entrants onto airline routes. See Steven T. Berry, *Estimating a Model of Entry in the Airline Industry*, 60 ECONOMETRICA, 889-917, (1993), for evidence. The airline industry constitutes one of the best examples where there are such objective criteria for identifying potential competitors.

97 John Kwoka & Evgenia Shumilkina, *The Price Effect of Eliminating Potential Competition: Evidence from an Airline Merger*, 58 JOURNAL OF INDUSTRIAL ECONOMICS 4, (2010).

98 Huubinh Le, *An Empirical Analysis of the Price and Output Effects of the Southwest/AirTran Merger*, 17 COMPETITION AND REGULATION IN NETWORK INDUSTRIES, 3-4, 226-240, (2016).

ined acquisitions among firms that account for more than 35,000 pharmaceutical drug projects, categorizing each project by its therapeutic category and mechanism of action.[99] They focus on cases where one company acquires another that has a directly overlapping project. In these cases, of course, the acquiring company has weaker incentives to continue development since it would cannibalize its own sales and profits, and indeed it may acquire the target company simply in order to kill off its development project. In its key finding, this study reports that acquired overlapping projects are 40 percent less likely to be continued in the development process after the merger than comparable non-acquired drugs or acquired non-overlapping drugs. These results make clear that so-called "killer acquisitions" in pharmaceuticals are both frequent and competitively harmful.

There are, to be sure, some distinctive practical difficulties in evaluating a merger with a threatening entrant that do not arise in mergers between incumbents. These difficulties begin with the threshold issue of identifying a potential competitor, since by definition such a firm does not currently operate in the market in question. In some cases, such as airlines, there may be objective criteria for identifying potential entrants; in other cases, company documents and third-party analyses may provide convincing evidence; and in yet other instances, market actions and reactions by the incumbent may signal its understanding of the threat posed by an outside firm. All of these methods pose challenges not faced in the simpler case of mergers involving incumbent competitors. Compounding these difficulties, while the theoretical framework for analyzing the competitive effect of a merger between an incumbent and a potential entrant is in principle analogous to that for a merger of incumbents, much of the now-standard apparatus for quantification—upward pricing pressure, event studies, merger simulation—is not applicable to the former.

All this has led to skepticism by the courts and caution by the enforcement agencies in making such cases. Court decisions have made it clear that challenges to such mergers have to clear an unusually high bar for proof. The relevant Supreme Court opinion stated that in order to challenge such an acquisition involving a potential competitor, several facts have to be established. It must be a concentrated market. The target firm must have the "characteristics, capabilities, and economic incentives to render it" a potential entrant. The targeted firm must be a unique potential entrant or at least one of very few well-positioned firms. And critically, there must be actual

---

99 Colleen Cunningham, Florian Ederer & Song Ma, *Killer Acquisitions*, (2018). SSRN: https://papers.ssrn.com/sol3/papers.cfm?abstract_id=3241707.

evidence that the target firm has "in fact tempered oligopolistic behavior" by incumbents.[100] This latter criterion, especially, is troublesome since it exceeds the standard for challenging a merger between incumbents. In addition, it overlooks entirely the case when the acquired company was considering entry, without the incumbent's knowledge.

The result of these stringent criteria has been few direct challenges to mergers involving potential competitors, although the antitrust agencies sometimes note concerns with potential competition as secondary matters in challenges brought primarily on other grounds.[101] Among the few examples of merger challenges on these grounds has been the FTC's opposition in 2002 to the acquisition by Questcor of the U.S. development rights to a synthetic alternative to its drug for treating certain serious infantile disorders.[102] Questcor had outbid rival purchasers in order to preserve its monopoly position, which it had then used to raise the drug's price from $40 to $34,000. The FTC required Questcor to license the rights to an approved buyer. More recently, the FTC sought to prohibit the acquisition of Synergy by Steris, arguing that Steris was otherwise likely to enter Synergy's market—contract sterilization of certain devices and products. Despite business documents clearly stating this, the court permitted the merger based on its belief that there were more potential entrants, a possibility that diminished Steris's unique importance.[103]

In another recent matter the FTC initially opposed the merger between Neilson and Arbitron, providers of measurement technologies for media viewing and listening, respectively. It approved the merger after securing an agreement that Arbitron would make a key technology available to third parties—other potential entrants—for a period of eight years.[104]

---

100 *U.S. v. Marine Bankcorporation*, 418 U.S. 602. Also, *U.S. v. Steris Corp.*, N.D. Ohio Sept. 24, 2015. See also, John Kwoka, *Non-Incumbent Competition: Mergers Involving Constraining and Prospective Competitors*, 52 Case W. Res. L. Rev., 173-209 (2001).

101 See, for example, the FTC complaint against Staples, *FTC v. Staples, Inc.*, available at https://www.ftc.gov/sites/default/files/documents/cases/1997/04/staples2; also, Statement of the Department of Justice regarding the proposed US Air-United Airlines merger, available at https://www.justice.gov/archive/atr/public/press_releases/2001/8701.htm.

102 FTC Complaint, https://www.ftc.gov/system/files/documents/cases/170118mallinckrodt_complaint_public, 2013.

103 For a discussion of this merger, see Jennifer Fauver & Subramaniam Ramanarayanan, *Challenges for Economic Analysis of Mergers Between Potential Competitors: Steris and Synergy*, 30 ANTITRUST (2016).

104 Statement of the FTC, Neilson Holdings & Arbitron, Sept. 2013.

One and only one firm accessed the technology, and when it introduced the resulting product, Neilsen promptly sued for infringement. In 2009 a similar agreement for technology access was obtained by the Department of Justice as a condition of allowing Google to acquire ITA.[105] This merger posed the added enforcement difficulty that it involved two firms, neither of which was active in the market in question—airline flight search—but both of which arguably might have entered.[106] As will be discussed in the next chapter, the efficacy of remedies in these cases is subject to some doubt.

These few agency challenges are dwarfed by the number of mergers and acquisitions involving firms with the potential to enter into an incumbent's business that are approved or never even evaluated for their competitive significance.[107] Many of these mergers involve extensions of product line-ups such as in rental cars or supermarkets, where modest current customer overlaps are used to justify acquisitions of firms not quite competing or not yet directly competing. Even if current product overlaps and customer diversion seem modest, of course, permitting such mergers can eliminate the most likely entrants and the most likely constraining outside firms. This can contribute to greater market power of incumbents without causing an increase in measured market concentration.

Other cases involve acquisitions of companies whose potential as entrants is harder to detect. This is especially the case in settings where the technology is fungible and its potential uses may be unknown even to the firm currently controlling it. These factors make it even more difficult to identify these so-called "nascent competitors." We shall have more to say about this in the discussion of the tech sector in Chapter 8.

Overall, there are compelling reasons and good evidence to support a reversal of the current accommodating posture toward mergers that eliminate potential competitors.

---

105 See Michael Topper, Stanley Watt & Marshall Yan, *Google-ITA: Creating a New Flight Search Competitor*, in THE ANTITRUST REVOLUTION, (J. Kwoka & L. White, eds., 6th edition 2014). This remedy will be discussed further below.

106 This is sometimes called a "potential potential-competition merger."

107 A recent such example would seem to be the proposed acquisitions of Bombardier and Embraer by Airbus and Boeing, respectively, just as the first two aircraft manufacturers launch larger planes that have become increasingly competitive with smallest aircraft produced by Boeing and Airbus. See Steven Perlstein, *Boeing and Airbus: The New 'Super-Duopoly'*, WASHINGTON POST, April 25, 2018.

RECOMMENDATIONS:

(1) The agencies must directly challenge mergers eliminating significant potential competitors to markets. Since the Supreme Court has created an undue burden on such enforcement, effective reform might require legislative action establishing that the same standards apply to these mergers as to those involving incumbents.

(2) The agencies should develop standards for enforcing the doctrine of potential competition. The standards should reflect considerations such as market concentration, the number of significant potential competitors, and relevant distinctions among them. A determination could be strengthened by, but not ultimately dependent on, documents or past experience, or by evidence of the outside firm's effect on the market or its consideration of entry.

(3) These standards must be included in revised Merger Guidelines and advocated by the agencies to the courts.

CHAPTER 6

REVISITING OTHER MERGER POLICY ISSUES:
Nonprice Effects, Monopsony, and Remedies

The preceding chapters have explained the basis for revising the significance attached to market structure and other factors in determining a merger's competitive effects. These issues are central to reforming merger control, but they do not constitute the entirety of what needs to be done, since a number of other important issues in merger control have been given inadequate attention over the past twenty-five years. This chapter will examine three dimensions of competition and policy that require rethinking.

The first of these concerns the nonprice effects of mergers. Despite the fact that some of these—such as quality and innovation—are often important dimensions of products and services, they have been given little formal attention in the guidelines or in merger control. The second issue—one that has been even more completely overlooked—is mergers that create or enhance market power on the buyer side. This so-called monopsony power is analogous to market power on the supply side but has drawn almost no policy attention. And finally, we note that merger enforcement has too often settled for remedies instead of challenges to competitively problematic mergers. But recent evidence has shown that these remedies have often not been effective, so that numerous anticompetitive mergers have been allowed to proceed with little or no effective constraints on the behavior of the merged firm.

This chapter will examine each of these critical areas of merger enforcement and offer necessary recommendations for reform.

6.1 Nonprice Outcomes

Attention in the Merger Guidelines is focused almost exclusively on the price effects of mergers. From market definition and measures of concentration to theories of harm and efficiencies, the framework and apparatus are geared to an examination of how a merger will likely alter market price. There is, of course, no question that attention to price is justified, but it is also indisputable that the various nonprice effects of mergers can be important as well. The effects of merger on quality, costs, variety, R&D and innovation are typically valued by consumers and they often represent important strategic variables to firms. The cursory treatment they get in the Merger Guidelines does not reflect their importance. One portion of comprehensive reform of merger control must therefore be further development and articulation of the analytical process and standards by which nonprice considerations are addressed in the evaluation of mergers.

The importance of nonprice factors is in principle clear, but less often appreciated is that in the case of some mergers, the adverse effects on nonprice dimensions can be at least as important as price. For example, in pharmaceuticals and the tech sectors, R&D and innovation outcomes are often critically important outcomes—sometimes perhaps more important than the price effect. They should be a primary focus of any review of the competitive effects of a merger. In video programming and distribution, characteristics such as variety, choice, and novelty are key considerations for consumers. In airlines, the effects of mergers on reliability, scheduling frequency and on-time performance are matters of concern, as well as price. In hospital mergers, health outcomes deservedly attract much attention. Moreover, in many cases price and quality effects may be interrelated, with merging parties claiming that higher price outcomes reflect improved service quality—flight frequency for airlines, reduced mortality for hospitals. In such cases a full evaluation of a merger may require examination of both price and quality, and the trade-off between the two.

It is striking, therefore, that the current treatment of nonprice issues in the guidelines does not reflect their importance. Remarkably, the 1982 Guidelines did not mention nonprice effects at all. The 1992 Merger Guidelines acknowledged the issue, but in a single sentence, buried in a footnote. That footnote—the entire policy guidance—reads as follows: "Sellers with market power also may lessen competition on dimensions other than price, such as product quality, service, or innovation." The 2010 update of the Merger Guidelines repeats that one-sentence statement and then adds the following assurance: "When the Agencies investigate whether a merger may lead to a substantial lessening of non-price competition, they employ an approach analogous to that used to evaluate price competition." They also include a brief subsection on innovation and product variety (more on which follows below).

These perfunctory statements provide no useful guidance with respect to the agencies' analytical approach to nonprice issues. Indeed, assurances about the analogy between nonprice and price analysis are misleading, if not incorrect, since the economics of nonprice effects differs from that for price. With respect to price, we normally expect high concentration to be associated with higher price and consumer harm, but the relevant economic theory and evidence regarding the effect of concentration and quality, variety, R&D, and technological change are more complex and the implications generally more ambiguous. For example, the effect of concentration on quality depends subtly on the way that different types of consumers value quality, and so the net effect of a merger may be either positive or negative.[108] In other cases, quality may be multidimensional so that even when consumer preferences for each dimension are not in dispute, combining multiple dimensions creates ambiguity. Similarly, a merger may create an additional product variant and consumer choice, but greater variety may be either excessive or beneficial depending on the underlying cost and utility functions.[109]

In some cases, the evaluation of quality may not pose great difficulties. For hospitals, for example, the evidence strongly suggests that mergers do not systematically either improve or worsen quality measured by a variety of specific health outcomes.[110] As a result, antitrust analysis of hospital mergers can focus simply on the price outcomes. In the case of airlines, the issue may be more complex since mergers at a minimum create greater single-line flight frequencies, although it appears to be the case that other service dimensions suffer. And in any event, valuing any such benefits poses considerable problems. While measuring the consumer benefit from a price change is relatively straightforward, there is nothing straightforward about measuring the value of greater seat selection options in airlines or better trained nursing staffs in hospitals.

One noteworthy attempt at that evaluation in the case of airlines has recently been set out by Israel et al.[111] That approach seeks to find an

---

108 Jean Tirole, THE THEORY OF INDUSTRIAL ORGANIZATION. MIT Press (1988).

109 For a simple exposition, see F.M. Scherer, *The Welfare Economics of Product Variety: An Application to the Ready-to-Eat Cereal Industry*, 28 JOURNAL OF INDUSTRIAL ECONOMICS 2, 113-13, (1979).

110 See, for example, David Balan, *A Retrospective Analysis of the Clinical Quality Effects of the Acquisition of Highland Park Hospital by Evanston Northwestern Healthcare*, 18 INTERNATIONAL JOURNAL OF THE ECONOMICS OF BUSINESS 1, 45-64 (2010).

111 Mark Israel, Bryan Keating, Daniel Rubinfeld & Robert Willig, *The Delta-Northwest Merger: Consumer Benefits from Airline Network Effects*, in THE ANTITRUST REVOLUTION, 6th ed. (Kwoka & White, eds., 2014).

equivalence between a quality increase and a price reduction, as follows: an improvement in quality such as flight frequency should increase quantity demanded, other things equal. Given that, there is a price decrease that alternatively could have caused that same increase in quantity. Then, under certain assumptions, the consumer benefit from that price decrease—which we know at least roughly how to measure—should be equivalent to the consumer benefit from the quality increase. While measuring these effects relies in part on facts specific to the airline industry, and while some of the underlying assumptions may not hold generally, this approach may be one useful starting point for assessing quality changes due to a merger.

A particularly important nonprice issue concerns innovation. It is well established that the impact of innovation on economic welfare is very substantial since growth of output may outweigh static inefficiencies from a merger in a relatively brief period of time. Moreover, innovation issues have become more prevalent in U.S. merger cases over the past twenty years. Gilbert reports that prior to 1995 few challenges mentioned innovation, whereas more than 20 percent of all challenges—and 90 percent of those in high tech industries—did so subsequently.[112]

Integrating innovation into merger analysis is therefore quite important, but unfortunately, the effects of concentration and mergers on innovation defy easy characterization. On the one hand, there are reasons to expect that a merger may favor innovation. These reasons include efficiencies from reduction of duplication, synergies from joining complementary functions, and greater opportunity for returns from innovation. There are experiences consistent with all of those possible benefits, but scenarios involving competitive harms from mergers are equally evident. Perhaps most obviously, if the merging firms have potentially competing products under development, one of the two projects may be slowed or altered or simply terminated in order to protect—indeed, enhance—future profits from the remaining project. Incentives to initiate development of entirely new products may also be diminished if both firms would have had a separate interest in doing so. As noted previously, there is evidence that mergers and acquisitions in the pharmaceutical sector have had precisely this effect.[113]

Compounding matters, economic theory indicates that the actual outcomes depend in complex ways on a number of other factors: the security of intellectual property rights, the nature and strength of spillovers, the

---

112 Rich Gilbert, INNOVATION MATTERS: COMPETITION POLICY FOR THE HIGH TECNOLOGY ECONOMY, MIT Press, forthcoming.

113 For recent confirmation of this concern, see Cunningham, op. cit.

probability of success in the R&D project, the strength of post-merger as well as pre-merger competition, product vs. process innovation, and entry barriers.[114] Several of these factors are difficult to operationalize. All are difficult to integrate into a single causal chain for purposes of merger evaluation analogous to that for price. And the empirical literature has not resolved these theoretical ambiguities. Studies report results in various directions, sometimes for reasons that are not entirely apparent. Some recent work even suggests that R&D intensity may reach its maximum value at some mid-level range of concentration, balancing favorable and unfavorable influences—although, as with much else, others dispute this interpretation.[115] Summaries of the few merger retrospectives on innovation (or for that matter, other nonprice effects) report no evidence of overall systematic effects, although there appears to be wide variation in the outcomes.[116]

In the face of this multitude of influential factors, it has proven difficult to set out a standard framework or methodology for evaluating the effects of a merger on innovation.[117] One framework that might seem helpful is the doctrine of potential competition. To the extent that the competitive concern involves the elimination of a near-term or potential competitive product or project, this would indeed be a useful approach. As presently formulated, however, this doctrine is not well suited to the task of addressing the more ambiguous scenarios involving pipeline projects, much less those at even more preliminary research stages where the competitive issues involve the capacity for research rather than identifiable products.

Another approach to analyzing innovation issues from mergers has been proposed by Gilbert & Sunshine.[118] They have advanced the concept

---

114 For a comprehensive analysis which I draw on here, see Gilbert, op. cit.

115 For evidence and a review, see Philippe Aghion, Nick Bloom, Richard Blundell, Rachel Griffith & Peter Howitt, *Competition and Innovation: An Inverted-U Relationship*, 120 QUARTERLY JOURNAL OF ECONOMICS 2, 701-728(2005).

116 See John Kwoka, *The Effects of Mergers on Innovation: Economic Framework and Empirical Evidence,*" in THE ROLES OF INNOVATION IN COMPETITION LAW ANALYSIS, (Edward Elgar, 2018). Also, John Kwoka & Shawn Kilpatrick, *Non-Price Effects of Mergers: Issues and Evidence*, 63 ANTITRUST BULLETIN 2, 169-182 (2018). This wide variation heightens the need to undertake an actual examination of each merger by itself.

117 Gilbert, for example, notes that "The complaints and supporting documents filed by the agencies in high-tech merger challenges rarely explain the mechanism by which the merger...would harm innovation." Gilbert, op. cit., forthcoming.

118 Rich Gilbert & Steven Sunshine, *Incorporating Dynamic Efficiency Concerns in Merger Analysis: The Use of Innovation Markets*, 63 ANTITRUST LAW JOURNAL 2, 569-601 (1995).

of an "innovation market" so that a merger affecting innovation competition would then arguably be scrutinized in the same manner as with respect to price. This construct, however, runs the risk of treating all innovation activity as fungible and hence defining that market too broadly. Yet another effort draws a parallel between the unilateral price effects of standard merger analysis and the similar unilateral effects from a merger to reduce the incentive to innovate. Some recent papers have modeled and developed the notion of "downward innovation pressure" from a reduction in innovation competition due to a merger.[119] This construct can in principle be modeled and its magnitude at least characterized. Moreover, it can be combined with the competitive effects of a merger with respect to price, potentially the basis for a wider synthesis of merger effects.

In summary, at present nonprice effects are not the focus of attention in many actual merger cases. Pricing is almost invariably the focus simply because the price effects of a merger are better understood, more easily modeled, and better measured. But that focus systematically underestimates the importance of nonprice effects, critically so for those mergers where innovation, quality, and variety are of key importance. For these reasons, the agencies need to better understand nonprice effects, better convey their importance in the guidelines, better equip themselves to bring relevant cases, and better argue the possible merger-related harms with respect to R&D and innovation, service quality, and product variety in specific contexts.

RECOMMENDATIONS:

> *(1) The agencies must set out the distinctive aspects of nonprice effects from mergers and incorporate these considerations in the Merger Guidelines or at least in some alternative policy commentary or guidance.*

---

119 See for example, Massimo Motta & E. Tarantino, *The Effect of Horizontal Mergers When Firms Compete in Prices and Investments*, Department of Economics and Business, Universitat Pompeu Fabra, Economics Working Paper No. 1579, 2017. Giulio Federico, Gregor Langus & Tommaso Valetti, *Horizontal Mergers and Product Innovation*, 59 INTERNATIONAL JOURNAL OF INDUSTRIAL ORGANIZATION C, 1-23 (2018). Important application of some of these principles is to be found in the DG Comp analysis of the merger of Dow and Dupont. In detailing the steps in its analysis of how innovative effort would likely be affected by the merger, it provides a roadmap for distinguishing and analyzing the likely competitive effects of a merger at various stages in the research and development chain. European Commission Decision, Annex 4, *Implications of the Economic Theory on Competition and Innovation in Light of the Features of the Transaction*, Brussels (March 27, 2017).

(2) *This guidance likely should be different according to each nonprice effect, such as quality, variety, and innovation, since the underlying economics and analytical approach for each differ. Their importance will depend on the merger in question.*

(3) *The agencies must challenge mergers based on nonprice effects of mergers whenever those are the dominant issue. It is essential to do so in order to restore vitality to these concerns and to persuade the judiciary of their importance.*

6.2 Monopsony Power

High on the list of antitrust issues that policy has not adequately addressed is market power by buyers, otherwise known as monopsony power. This arises when a buyer of some good or service—for example, labor services required for some production process—represents such a large fraction of demand for that input that its purchases alter market price. In that case the buyer increases its profit by limiting its purchases below the competitive level, in order to suppress the price it pays on all units. This market distortion is analogous to the distortion from market power on the selling side, with its higher price and lower quantity. Despite this close analogy, monopsony power as a possible consequence of mergers has received far less attention than it should.

The reasons for this oversight are not altogether clear. Some have speculated that this is due to the antitrust focus on "consumer welfare," which suggests harm to final consumers of some product rather than harms to sellers of inputs.[120] Or it may reflect a belief that "company towns" and other isolated input markets were things of the past. Whatever truth there may have been to this belief, the vast consolidation of U.S. industries has restructured local input markets as well as broader output markets, arguably enhancing buyer power in some regions and for some inputs.[121]

Whatever the reasons for this oversight, the appropriate policy and tools for addressing mergers for monopsony and for monopoly would seem in principle to mirror each other. Analysis of possible monopsony power would begin by defining an input market and a geographic market within which buyers possess market power. For the same reasons as for monopoly, buyer

---

120 For discussion, see Suresh Naidu, Eric Posner & E. Glen Weyl, *Antitrust Remedies for Labor Market Power*, 132 HARVARD LAW REVIEW, 549-600 (2018).

121 Consider, for example, Amazon Fulfillment Centers, by design located in less populated areas where alternative employment opportunities are correspondingly scarce.

concentration could be measured and other tools of modern merger analysis, including pricing pressure and simulation techniques, could be applied.[122]

Yet while the framework would be familiar, the application would involve some significant differences.[123] The relevant antitrust market for monopsony, for example, would consist of a geographic region within which a small number of buyers account for a large fraction of purchases of some well-defined material or labor or other input. Thus, if most nurses in some city work for one of two local hospitals, the merger of those hospitals would eliminate competition between the hospitals for nurses and arguably result in a reduction in their wages and harm to the competitive operation of the "local market for nurses." What is sometimes overlooked is that this effect does not depend on whether there is any increase in prices to final consumers of hospital services.[124] Similarly, if a merger combined the dominant meat packers in a region, a merger between them could enhance their buying power over local farmers with limited alternatives for sale of their livestock, again, regardless of whether the merged meat packer competed in its product market with many other meat packers that were located elsewhere.

An additional distinction that needs to be emphasized is that between input price reductions due to monopsony power versus reductions resulting from changes in bargaining power or lower transactions costs. Changes in bargaining power between a buyer and a seller can change the split in surplus and be reflected in a change in transactions price. If that does not affect quantity, however, there is no efficiency effect. On the other hand, a true reduction in transactions cost is an efficiency gain, but not one due to market power. Operationalizing monopsony power resulting from a merger requires carefully drawing these distinctions.

---

122 For discussion, see Ioana Marinescu & Herbert Hovenkamp, *Anticompetitive Mergers in Labor Markets*, FACULTY SCHOLARSHIP AT PENN LAW, 1031-1063 (2019). Also, Carl Shapiro, *Protecting Competition in the American Economy: Merger Control, Tech Titans, Labor Markets*, 33 JOURNAL OF ECONOMIC PERSPECTIVES 3, 69-93 (2019).

123 These distinctions are discussed in Scott Hemphill & Nancy L. Rose, MERGERS THAT HARM SELLERS, 127 YALE LAW JOURNAL 7, 1742-2203 (2018).

124 Indeed, there is no particular reason why the input market would correspond to the output market in which those firms operate, nor for that matter, any reason why they operate in the same output market at all. A Texas case against a no-poaching agreement illustrates this point. The two companies charged with suppressing local wages were eBay and Intuit, clearly non-competitors in their outputs, but major purchasers of "specialized computer engineers and scientists" in the area. This example is cited in Marinescu et al., op. cit.

The 2010 Merger Guidelines do include a brief section on mergers between competing buyers. They state that such mergers "can enhance market power on the buying side of the market, just as mergers of competing sellers can enhance market power on the selling side of the market" and that the agencies employ "essentially the [same] framework" to evaluate both sides of the market. Despite this language, the agencies have brought very few cases based on input market effects. The exception is the FTC complaint against the merger of Grifols and Biotest.[125] The agency alleged that the companies were the only buyers of human source plasma in several cities where, as a result of the merger, they would be able to reduce the fees paid to donors.

In another case the Justice Department sued to prevent the merger between JBS and National Beef Packing in 2008.[126] The DOJ alleged that as a result of the merger, the parties would be able to reduce the price they paid for "fed cattle" —cattle ready for slaughter—in two regions of the country. The parties abandoned that merger. DOJ also filed suit against the proposed merger of Tysons Foods and Hillshire Farms alleging that the combination of two buyers of sows from farmers would result in lower purchase price.[127] Subject to a modest divestiture, that 2014 merger was allowed to proceed.

These few challenges are outweighed by the large number of mergers that have resulted in substantial increases in buyer concentration in agricultural markets over the past twenty-five years.[128] The percentage of hogs processed by the four largest meatpackers nearly doubled, to 66 percent, between 1980 and 2014. Four-buyer concentration for cattle rose from 55 to 79 percent, and for poultry from 34 to 57 percent. In field crops, the largest four wet corn millers and separately the largest four soybean processors account for more than 80 percent of their respective markets. The result in these and other markets is that farmers face increasingly limited alternative buyers for their crops and livestock, with predictable effects on prices.[129]

There has been considerable recent attention to the exercise of monopsony power in labor markets, although the focus of attention has been on

125 *FTC v. Grifols, S.A., and Grifols Shared Service*, November 2018.

126 https://www.justice.gov/atr/case-document/complaint-137.

127 https://www.justice.gov/atr/case-document/final-judgment-182.

128 Zoe Willingham & Andy Green, A Fair Deal for Farmers, Center for American Progress, May 2019.

129 See also, Clarie Kelloway & Sarah Miller, "Food and Power: Addressing Monopolization in America's Food System," Open Markets Institute, March 2019, and Peter Carstensen, "Concentration and the Destruction of Competition in Agricultural Markets: The Case for Change in Public Policy," Wisc. L. Rev. 2001, and Competition Policy and the Control of Buyer Power, Edwin Elgar, 2017.

no-poaching and noncompete agreements rather than mergers. Ashenfelter & Krueger have documented the frequency of such restrictions, reporting no-poaching clauses—which prohibit employers from hiring each other's employees—in more than half of all 158 large franchise agreements that they surveyed.[130] A 2106 Issue Brief from the Council of Economic Advisors identified non-compete agreements as one factor reducing worker wages and contributing to the decline in labor's share of national income.[131] In that same year, the FTC and DOJ issued a joint Antitrust Guidance for Human Resources Professionals which cautioned that "Agreements among employers not to recruit certain employees or not to compete on certain terms of employment are illegal."[132] The agencies, however, have taken few actions against such restrictions. One exception has been the DOJ's successful challenge to agreements involving Apple, Google, Intuit, Intel, Pixar, Lucasfirm, and eBay that they not make "cold call" contacts seeking possibly to hire away each other's employees.[133]

Again, while these latter matters are not mergers, they do signal interest by the antitrust agencies in monopsony practices. That said, considerably more needs to be done in order to bring attention to the possible distortionary effects from mergers that create or enhance buyer power.

RECOMMENDATIONS:

(1) *The discussion of mergers between competing buyers in the Merger Guidelines needs more development with respect to several issues. These include the distinctive features of geographic market definition (e.g., labor mobility), possible entry by new input buyers, and other issues.*

(2) *While the guidelines note the distinction between lower input prices due to monopsony power versus lower prices due to reductions in transactions costs and perhaps due to changes in bargaining, operational criteria for these distinctions need to be provided.*

---

130 Orley Ashenfelter & Alan Krueger, *Theory and Evidence on Employer Collusion in the Franchise Sector*, (NBER Working Paper No. 24831, 2018).

131 White House Council of Economic Advisors, Labor Market Monopsony: Trends, Consequences and Policy Responses 4 (Issue Brief, October 2016).

132 U.S. Department of Justice Antitrust Division & Federal Trade Commission, Antitrust Guidance for Human Resource Professionals (Oct. 20, 2016).

133 Press Release, U.S. Dep't of Justice, Justice Department Requires Six High Tech Companies to Stop Entering into Anticompetitive Employee Solicitation Agreements (September 24, 2010).

(3) Merger policy needs to move expeditiously to catch up with the actual exercise of monopsony power resulting from mergers.

6.3 Fixing Merger Remedies

Few challenges to mergers result in actual litigation.[134] Parties may abandon or modify a proposed merger upon notification of a likely challenge, but increasingly the agencies enter into settlements of prospective litigation through some type of remedy that allows the merger in part or whole to proceed while subjecting it to conditions intended to protect competition. There is, however, increasing evidence that these remedies are often not effective in resolving competitive concerns with mergers and may, in addition, impose continuing administrative burdens on the agencies. As a result, a necessary component of merger control reform is for the agencies to substantially reduce reliance on merger remedies. This applies with special force for those remedies known as conduct or behavioral remedies. The agencies should study carefully the circumstances under which these remedies have a predictably high probability of succeeding, and be prepared to challenge other anticompetitive mergers rather than devising problematic methods for allowing mergers to proceed.

The theory that underlies a classic merger remedy is simple and appealing: where a large and complex merger creates competitive concerns in a limited area of the merging firms' operations, antitrust policy can require divestiture of one of the overlapping products to a qualified buyer, thereby fixing that specific concern while permitting the remaining operations of the companies to merge.[135] This policy preserves the same number of independent and capable entities, each with its own profit-maximizing incentives intact, as before the merger. Economics would therefore predict that firms would conduct themselves in ways that should lead to a market equilibrium similar to the pre-merger outcome. These structural remedies have long been used by the antitrust agencies and have generally met with a fair degree of success. While careful study could improve their success rates, divestitures have a constructive role to play in merger control.

There is, however, a second type of remedy that more recently the agencies have employed with greater frequency. These so-called conduct or behavioral remedies permit a merger to proceed in its entirety but seek to pre-

---

134 While there are about 50 merger investigations in any year, on average about one or two actual cases go to trial.

135 See *MMCR*. Also, John Kwoka, *Merger Remedies: An Incentives/Constraints Framework*, 62 ANTITRUST BULLETIN 2, 367-381 (2017).

vent the merged firm from engaging in specific anticompetitive acts. Thus, the remedy may prohibit divisions of the merged company from exchanging competitively sensitive information that would otherwise not be available to an independent company. Or it may impose a requirement to supply a rival with some input that previously had been supplied by an entity that is now part of the merged company with which the rival competes. Conduct remedies are fundamentally different from divestitures in that they require actions by the merged firm that are inconsistent with its profit-maximizing objectives. Thus, they run counter to the firm's own incentives, rather than relying on those incentives in order to achieve the purposes of the remedy. Not surprisingly, therefore, the record of conduct remedies is not favorable.[136]

These two types of remedies—divestitures and conduct approaches—each have limitations that have been analyzed in economics and confirmed in the course of recent policy actions. In the case of divestitures, it has long been understood that for them to be effective, it is crucially important that the divested operation not simply be the product or operation in question but also include crucial supply or distribution arrangements, product development capabilities, etc.[137] In addition, the buyer must have the financial and operational capabilities to integrate and operate the divested assets fully. Since the merging parties have no incentives to ensure this, even in the most ordinary of divestitures, the agencies must be on guard against strategic choices put forward by the firms.

Beyond that, recent policy has taken this standard model of divestitures into new directions for which the same favorable outcomes are much less likely to hold. One such direction concerns the sheer scale of divestitures, that is, the extent of divested assets. The FTC's remedy for the *Teva-Allegan* pharmaceutical merger, for example, involved divestiture not of a single or a few overlapping products, but rather divestiture of 87 specific overlapping products.[138] The overlap comprised significant fractions of

---

136 These are often used when structural remedies—that is, divestitures—are infeasible, or as supplementary conditions to divestiture remedies. For these reasons, conduct remedies have often been used in cases of vertical mergers, but their limitations remain the same. There also are "hybrid" remedies involving both structural and conduct elements.

137 For an early statement of this, see FTC , *A Study of the Commission's Divestiture Process*, https://www.ftc.gov/sites/default/files/documents/reports/study-commissions-divestiture-process/divestiture_0.pdf (1999).

138 Press release, U.S. FTC, FTC Requires Teva to Divest Over 75 Generic Drugs to Settle Competition Concerns Related to its Acquisition of Allergan's Generic Business https://www.ftc.gov/news-events/press-releases/2016/07/ftc-requires-teva-divest-over-75-generic-drugs-rival-firms-settle. For discussion, see J. Kwoka (2017), op. cit.

each merging firm's product portfolio, so that the divestiture effectively restructured the firms and transformed the industry they operated in. It also transformed several smaller companies that acquired various subsets of the divested products. And it raised the ultimate question of whether this vast rearrangement of industry assets—itself more like M&A work—resulted in the preservation of competition, since the remedy had far wider effects than on a single product or a single firm.

A second way in which divestitures have recently ventured onto new and problematic ground has involved cases where the divested asset or assets are insufficient to create an equivalent new competitor and so the agencies have sought to find and integrate other assets in order to create a stronger new entity. In this shift from simply divesting assets to combining assets in order to create an effective competitor, the competition agency has embarked on quite a different task, one requiring insight into the internal operation of firms, rather than simply their external properties. Some examples illustrate the issues. In its investigation of the proposed merger of U.S. Foods and Sysco, for many months the FTC labored over the unlikely argument that a much smaller regional food distributor could grow and enter other regional markets across the country and thereby become a major national player adequate to replace the merged firm. The same was the case with respect to Staples's proposal to acquire the remaining office superstore, Office Depot/Office Max in 2010. The FTC sought to determine whether a regional office supplier could, with some divestitures from the merging parties, become a second truly national player to replace that eliminated by merger. Both of those mergers were eventually opposed because the supposed replacement firms were ultimately not viewed as sufficient entrants, but only after long and serious investigations of what would seem implausible on its face—an agency brokered re-arrangement of industry operations and assets to construct a new full-blown competitor.

A more recent case illustrates the dangers of seeking to create a new rival for the express purpose of entering markets where a merger would result in competitive harms. The proposed merger of Sprint and T-Mobile was approved by DOJ based entirely on developing a new entrant into the national wireless market to replace that the competition lost due to the merger. This new entrant would be Dish—currently a satellite television provider without wireless experience or assets but which is supposed to become a new fully effective competitor by combining Sprint's divested prepaid business plus some of the merged firm's stores and cell towers and its own spectrum assets and thereby build a nationwide competitive alternative service from scratch. Crucially, at each stage Dish would be dependent on the merged firm for support services, on-going technical assistance, and even for the actual wireless service itself, despite the obvious fact that the merged company has no incentive to do so in a full and timely manner. And even if this all were to work, Dish would not be expected to emerge as a standalone rival for at least seven years.[139]

The remedy for the *Sprint/T-Mobile* merger in fact is more illustrative of a conduct remedy, which permits a merger to go forward while requiring the merged firm to act in ways contrary to its own interests. These remedies seek to constrain the merged company from taking anticompetitive actions or require that it help rivals in ways that diminish the merged firm's own profits. Such remedies are necessarily difficult to write and difficult to enforce. They must, for example, fully specify the prohibited conduct in all possible circumstances both at present and into the future. They suffer from acute informational asymmetries that put the agencies at a major disadvantage in identifying possible violations. Success requires overriding the merged company's incentives to avoid or evade any constraints on its profit-maximizing behavior. Moreover, once in place, the antitrust agencies are ill equipped to engage in what is essentially regulatory oversight.

Despite these problems, about ten years ago the Justice Department adopted a more favorable view of conduct remedies. It issued a Remedies Guide that endorsed their use in a wider set of circumstances and proceeded to employ such remedies in several high-profile cases.[140] This more expansive use of conduct remedies—and their inherent limitations—are illustrated by several major merger settlements of that time. In the *Comcast-NBCU* merger, for example, the settlement included a provision that sought to require the integrated company to continue to provide video programming to rival cable distributors on "economically equivalent terms."[141] That criterion, unobjectionable by itself, required further explanation of what constituted "economically equivalent terms," but the definition of that phrase makes its inherent limitations clear.

---

139 John Kwoka, *Masquerading as Merger Control: The U.S. Department of Justice Settlement with Sprint and T-Mobile*, AMERICAN ANTITRUST INSTITUTE (August 2019) https://www.antitrustinstitute.org/wp-content/uploads/2019/08/Kwoka_Sprint-TMobile-Settlenent_8.21.19_F.pdf.

140 U.S. DEP'T OF JUSTICE, ANTITRUST DIVISION POLICY GUIDE TO MERGER REMEDIES (June 2011), https://www.justice.gov/sites/default/files/atr/legacy/2011/06/17/272350.pdf. This guide was a revision of an earlier guide that took an appropriately skeptical view of conduct remedies. See also Diana Moss & John Kwoka, *Behavioral Merger Remedies: Evaluation and Implications for Antitrust Enforcement*, 57 ANTITRUST BULLETIN 4, 979-1011 (2012).

141 Rogerson, op. cit., 2019.

'Economically equivalent' means the price, terms, and conditions that, in the aggregate, reasonably approximate those on which the Defendants provide Video Programming to an MVPD [multichannel video program distributor, e.g., cable company], and shall take account of, among other things, any difference in advertising revenues earned by Defendants through...[online video] distribution and those earned through MVPD distribution; any limitation of Defendants' legal rights to provide Video Programming as a linear feed over the Internet or other IP-based transmission path; any generally applicable, market-based requirements regarding minimum subscriber and penetration rates; and any other evidence concerning differences in revenues earned by Defendants in connection with the provision of Video Programming to [online video distribution] rather than the MVPD.

This definition requires somehow combining the incommensurate—"price, terms, and conditions"—into some "aggregate," that "reasonably approximate[s]" some other such combination. In addition, it is subject to allowances for further incommensurate differences in advertising revenues, legal rights, any other "generally applicable" marketing benchmarks, plus "any other evidence" of certain revenue differences. Such conditions are open-ended and ambiguous; they are likely to provoke endless controversy; and they are ultimately deferential to the merged company, which can better provide an explanation for its practices than the outside company can demonstrate its anticompetitive intent and effects.

Other efforts to construct conduct remedies have encountered similar problems.[142] The settlement of the merger between Ticketmaster and Live Nation sought to prevent the merged company from using its dominant position in ticketing services to force independents to utilize its other services. Language in the order was intended to prevent the merged company from retaliating against independents that refused to accept other services as a condition of using Ticketmaster's ticketing services, with a definition of "retaliation" that relied in part on the "purpose" of certain actions taken by the integrated company. Persistent doubts about this remedy were confirmed by the Justice Department's subsequent action against the merged companies. In 2020 DOJ acknowledged that the order had failed to prevent the company from the prohibited actions and modified

---

142 For discussion of several, see John Kwoka, *The Promise and Perils of Conduct Remedies in Merger Review*, forthcoming.

the original order by "clarifying" some language that Ticketmaster used to evade its obvious intent. Regardless of the efficacy of the new remedy, Ticketmaster achieved its anticompetitive goals for nearly a decade.[143] A similarly dubious remedy for the merger of Google and ITA sought to prohibit the exchange of competitively sensitive information between the parties through the use of a so-called firewall. The remedy, however, explicitly allowed the transfer of personnel from one division to the other even if the individual possessed such information so long as that person had not committed that information to their memories deliberately for the purpose of information transfer.[144]

It is difficult to believe that such remedies were devised with the expectation that they would be effective. There is considerable evidence that remedies are often ineffective. The first relevant study was due to the Federal Trade Commission itself in 1999, and that agency conducted a second study just two years ago.[145] Both of these examined that agency's experience with remedies (primarily divestitures), relied on interviews more than on data, and focused on whether divested assets remained in the market rather than whether competition had been preserved. Nonetheless, and despite some other flaws, these studies found that a substantial fraction of remedies failed even that test.[146] In addition, my research has examined the effects of all the remedies used in the mergers for which retrospectives have been conducted. This research found that mergers subject to divestitures resulted in price increases of about 5.6 percent, little different from mergers that were outright cleared. While the number of studied conduct remedy cases was very small, they resulted in an average price increase in excess of 13 percent.[147] In recent years, DOJ has withdrawn a 2011 Remedies Guide that expressed a greater willingness to use conduct remedies, and both agencies have declared their determination to exercise more caution in their use of remedies generally, and to avoid reliance on conduct remedies in particular.[148]

---

143 "Justice Department Will Move to Significantly Modify and Extend Consent Decree with Live Nation/Ticketmaster," Dec. 19, 2019. See also John Kwoka, Conduct Remedies, with 2020 Hindsight: Have We Learned Anything in the Last Decade?, CPI ANTITRUST CHRONICLE, April 2020, Vol. 1(1), pp. 12-17.

144 Kwoka, *The Promise and Perils,* n. 143.

145 U.S. FTC Divestiture Study, op. cit. See also "The FTC's Merger Remedies 2006-2012," 2017.

146 The second FTC study had numerous methodological defects that invalidated several of its major conclusions. See Appendix B for my analysis.

147 *MMCR,* as corrected.

148 U.S. Senate Commerce Committee, *Joseph Simons Completed Initial Questionnaire,* (Feb. 2018). Makin Delrahim, Modernizing the Merger Review Process, Remarks at the Global Antitrust Forum, (Sept. 25, 2018).

These experiences and evidence make clear that remedies overall should be used sparingly and conduct remedies scarcely at all. Beyond that, some recent proposals for modification and improvement deserve attention. One suggestion would seek to identify the specific conditions under which remedies are more vs. less likely to be effective.[149] For example, conduct remedies would appear more likely effective when they impose restraints that are ancillary rather than central to the firm's operations(since the latter would give the firm maximum incentive to avoid them), when they are of relatively short duration so as to minimize opportunities for evasion, and when they have specific metrics for success. Studies of the relevant conditions would be an important undertaking for the agencies.

A second set of proposals would alter the terms of remedies themselves. Remedies could be subjected to mid-course or even *ex post* modification where they are found to be demonstrably unsuccessful.[150] Another proposal is to impose sufficiently large fines to render violations of remedy orders unprofitable, as has been done with some success in other jurisdictions.[151] A further proposal, suggested by the Assistant Attorney General for Antitrust, would be to "bifurcate trials" into phases evaluating the transaction and another phase focusing on the remedy, so as to make clear the distinctive issues and burden of each inquiry.[152]

A third proposal that should be considered is to unwind mergers that were approved on the basis of remedies that ultimately failed to restore or preserve competition. While challenging a consummated merger on these grounds raises several practical issues, this policy would make clear that a remedy accompanying merger approval is in fact approval conditional on an effective remedy. This would diminish merging companies' premerger incentives to negotiate language they know will be easily evaded, and their post-merger incentives to avoid the intent of the remedy.

Overall the implication of these considerations is that remedies have been used too often, too widely, too optimistically, too casually, and perhaps

---

149 See J. Kwoka, *MMCR* for suggestions.

150 Steven Salop, *Modifying Merger Consent Decrees to Improve Merger Enforcement Policy*, 31 ANTITRUST 1, 15-20 (2016).

151 The European Union has imposed penalties on occasion running into billions of euros, large enough to get the attention of even the biggest tech companies for violations. On the other hand, it is not clear that formal violations are the most common problem; rather, it appears more often that the remedy as written can be evaded or avoided.

152 Gary Arlen, *DOJ, FTC Officials Spar over Roles in Antitrust Reviews*, MULTI-CHANNEL NEWS, March 21, 2019.

even strategically to the extent that they represent methods of avoiding challenging mergers but wishing to appear to be taking some action. This overuse of remedies, especially conduct remedies, must be reversed in order to reverse the unfortunate evolution of merger policy into remedy policy.

RECOMMENDATIONS:

> *(1) Merger policy needs to challenge anticompetitive mergers in all cases except where circumstances predictably justify the use of remedies. The necessary conditions for remedies should be narrowly construed and specified in policy documents.*

> *(2) Conduct remedies in particular must be avoided except for very unusual cases where merger benefits are large and indisputable, where there is no alternative, and where conditions for their success are fully satisfied. Otherwise, the merger should be challenged.*

> *(3) The agencies need to monitor the outcomes of remedies, impose fines and other penalties for non-compliance, and intervene if necessary after the fact in order to restore market competition.*

CHAPTER 7

REVIEWING BROADER ISSUES: Vertical Mergers, Common Ownership, and Tech

The preceding list of issues covers a number of major reforms necessary for horizontal merger control to reflect modern economics and to revive its important place in public policy. There are, however, other issues that either substantially overlap with or represent important extensions of horizontal merger control. The first of these involves vertical mergers, that is, mergers of firms in successive stages of production. The second analyzes the growing concern over third-party or common ownership of firms in an industry as an alternative to mergers among them. And finally, we examine the numerous mergers and acquisitions in the tech sector, which is one of several issues prompted by the rise of these companies.

Discussion here will focus on mergers, recognizing that each of these topics has dimensions beyond mergers that are not taken up here. In tech, for example, these other issues include control over data, adequacy of privacy protections, and abuse of platforms for antisocial purposes as well as competition concerns. [153] A similar focus on mergers and horizontal competition will guide our discussions of common ownership and of vertical mergers. This approach will suggest a number of recommendations for each of these topics that will substantially strengthen antitrust generally.

7.1 Vertical Mergers and Their Horizontal Effects

Firms in successive stages of production do not, by definition, compete in the same market and as a result, mergers between them do not by

---

153 To be sure, these are not entirely distinct, since greater size from merger can enhance a company's ability to extract further advantages through some of these contractual provisions. For comprehensive discussions of these competitive concerns, see Report, Chancellor of the Exchequer, UK, Unlocking Digital Competition: Report of the Expert Panel (March 2019); also Report, Stigler Committee on Digital Platforms (May 2019), and Report to the EU, Competition Policy for the Digital Era, 2019.

themselves raise concentration in either of the markets in which they operate. But some vertical mergers can serve to create, enhance, exploit, or defend horizontal market power by the merging firms. For much of the past forty years, however, the dominant view was different: as espoused by the Chicago school, vertical integration and, by analogy, vertical mergers were said rarely if ever to cause competitive harm. It was further argued that vertical mergers were nearly certain to produce efficiencies from the elimination of double marginalization and other cost savings.

Both of these propositions have now been shown to be altogether incorrect or at least dependent on strong assumptions. The result has been a history of too quick and often erroneous dismissal of the potential of vertical mergers to harm competition and consumers. While the antitrust consequences of vertical mergers are now being evaluated somewhat more carefully and critically by the agencies, the analytical issues remain less well developed, and agency scrutiny and judicial acceptance remain well behind that for horizontal mergers. This needs to be rectified.

There are several theories of competitive harm from vertical mergers that are now well recognized in economics.[154] The focus of most recent attention is on foreclosure, a strategy by which the integrated firm disadvantages an independent rival at one stage, where the rival has a business dependence on the integrated firm. Foreclosure comes in two forms—customer foreclosure and input foreclosure.[155]

Input foreclosure arises when a firm that had previously supplied critical inputs to independent downstream firms integrates with one of those downstream firms. After integration, the merged firm no longer has the same incentives to continue supplying other downstream firms on the same terms, since those other firms are direct competitors to its own downstream division. Accordingly, the vertically integrated firm predictably raises the price of that critical input, or supplies it on less advantageous terms, in order to diminish the degree of competition it faces at that stage.[156]

---

154 See, for example, Steven Salop & David Culley, *Potential Competitive Effects of Vertical Mergers: A How-To Guide for Practitioners* (December 8, 2014) SSRN: https://ssrn.com/abstract=2522179.

155 For the seminal contribution, see Patrick Rey & Jean Tirole, "A Primer on Foreclosure," in HANDBOOK OF INDUSTRIAL ORGANIZATION (M. Armstrong & R. Porter eds., 2006. Also, Steven Salop, *Reinvigorating Vertical Merger Enforcement*, 127 YALE LAW JOURNAL 7, 1742-2203 (2018).

156 These strategies collectively are termed foreclosure, thus including a wider array that outright refusal to deal.

Customer foreclosure reflects the same compromised incentives of the vertically integrated firm when it is a customer of suppliers with which, as a result of the merger, it competes. It becomes more profitable for the now vertically integrated firm to exclude independent suppliers from its purchase decisions, or at least to drive down the price it pays. As with input foreclosure, this anticompetitive strategy is made possible by vertical integration, which gives the merged firm a measure of control over its direct rivals. Indeed, it is fair to say that any vertical merger in which one or both firms are of significant size in their market raises the possibility of foreclosure against an independent rival at either stage.

While these foreclosure possibilities have long arisen in some vertical mergers, it is only recently that they have begun to receive serious attention by the agencies. The enforcement record is weak. Input foreclosure was the key element in Comcast's purchase of NBCU, since the latter's Universal Studios division contained a vast library of movie content that the merged company might no longer make available to rival video distributors.[157] Similarly, the Justice Department's recent challenge to the merger of AT&T and Time Warner rested in part on the concern that Time Warner's content might be withheld from rivals of AT&T's DirecTV video distribution division.[158] The first of these was settled with a remedy of doubtful effectiveness, as already discussed, while the second was litigated, but unsuccessfully, by the Justice Department.

Customer foreclosure has also been a concern in several recent mergers and proposed mergers in the same video programming and distribution sector. The proposed merger of Comcast-NBCU and Time Warner Cable in 2014, for example, would have substantially increased the merged company's position as a national distributor and therefore as a purchaser of video programming. It was likely to alter its program purchasing decisions in favor of its own programming, adversely affecting the supply from competing sources.[159] This merger was abandoned in the face of opposition by the Federal Communications Commission.

---

157 William Rogerson, *A Vertical Merger in the Video Programming and Distribution Industry: Comcast-NBCU*, in THE ANTITRUST REVOLUTION, (J. Kwoka & L. White, eds., 6th edition 2014). Also, William Rogerson, "Economic Theories of Harm Raised by the Proposed Comcast/TWC Transaction," in THE ANTITRUST REVOLUTION (J. Kwoka & L. White, eds., 7th ed., 2019).

158 Complaint, *U.S. v. AT&T*, Case 1:17-cv-02511 (Nov. 20, 2017), https://www.justice.gov/atr/case-document/file/1012916. Full disclosure: I consulted with the Justice Department on this merger.

159 To be clear, the merger raised other competitive issues. Full disclosure: I consulted for Entravision in opposition to this merger.

In addition to foreclosure, there are other competitive concerns with vertical integration, concerns that work through different channels but still affect horizontal competition. One of these involves potential competition. Since vertically related firms likely know much about each other's businesses, each may also be the most likely entrant into the other's business. A vertical merger simultaneously eliminates both the threat of entry into the upstream and the threat of entry into the downstream market in one stroke.

Yet another possible effect of a vertical merger may be to increase the barriers to entry by any other firm into either of the now-merged markets. The reason is that a firm threatening or contemplating entry into either market by itself may, post-merger, find that it must compete against an integrated firm offering a bundle of two products. Without the ability to offer the second product or the same bundle, the potential entrant faces a higher barrier to entry and operation. This "two-market entry barrier" has been noted in past guidelines but, despite its obvious importance, no longer appears as an explicit competitive issue in recent versions of the guidelines.[160]

On the other hand, under certain circumstances vertical integration can indeed produce various offsetting efficiencies recognizable under antitrust standards. Some of these are operating efficiencies—savings in transactions cost, improved coordination, and so forth—that arise from replacing market-based transactions with internal administrative operation. These are generally difficult to prove, much less to measure. Another widely cited efficiency derives from the elimination of double marginalization. This effect occurs when both premerger stages independently mark up their products. The result is that the downstream stage marks up the already marked-up input, creating a diseconomy that simultaneously reduces total profits of the two firms, and by reducing output, harms consumers as well. Vertical integration can avoid this double marginalization, and thereby benefit both consumers and firms.

This latter "efficiency" lay at the core of the Chicago school case for vertical integration, although more recent work has shown the proposition to be less generally applicable and its benefits less straightforward than commonly asserted.[161] For example, double marginalization can be avoided by

---

160 "Two-market entry" was noted in the original 1982 Merger Guidelines in a section marked "Non-Horizontal Mergers" and now commonly known as the Vertical Merger Guidelines. This competitive concern has been omitted from the new draft Vertical Merger Guidelines.

161 John Kwoka & Margaret Slade, *Second Thoughts on Double Marginalization*, ANTITRUST, forthcoming. SSRN (Sept. 13, 2019), https://papers.ssrn.com/sol3/papers.cfm?abstract_id=3452207.

the simple expedient of a properly structured two-price contract—a fairly routine device in many businesses.[162]   Moreover, the elimination of double marginalization does not actually reduce marginal cost—the classic merger-related efficiency—but rather is a pecuniary economy that may, under some circumstances, increase output.

For those vertical mergers that do pose significant competitive concerns, there has been little formal guidance for the agencies and courts to rely upon.[163]   By one count, there have been 56 vertical mergers reviewed by DOJ and FTC in the period from 1994 until 2018.[164]   Of those, only one was challenged outright—the *AT&T-Time Warner* case—and another six were abandoned. The remaining 51 were approved, typically with some conduct remedy. Given the frequency and importance of such mergers, their ambiguous economic effects, and the weakness of conduct remedies, this record indicates a policy failure.

One possible framework for strengthening enforcement is proposed to Baker et al.[165] Their approach recommends there be no presumption that vertical mergers benefit competition, that efficiency claims be critically evaluated, that any safe harbor should be avoided, and that consideration should be given to a presumption against vertical mergers under certain conditions. These circumstances include the above-mentioned concerns with customer and input foreclosure and with the elimination of potential competition or a maverick firm. Baker et al. would also tighten the standard in the case of vertical mergers by dominant platform companies, as will be discussed below.[166]

---

162 This was precisely the reason that the FCC rejected the parties claims of efficiency from eliminating double marginalization in the *Comcast-NBCU* merger.

163 The 1984 Non-horizontal Merger Guidelines addressed vertical mergers, but it is widely agreed that these are outdated and have long been ignored.

164 Salop & Culley, *supra* note 154.

165 Jonathan B. Baker, Nancy Rose, Steven Salop & Fiona Scott Morton, "Five Principles for Vertical Merger Enforcement Policy," Antitrust, Summer 2019.

166 As this is written, the FTC and DOJ have issued draft vertical merger guidelines. However welcome are such guidelines in principle, these describe a considerably narrower view of competitive concerns with such mergers. They recognize one but not both forms of foreclosure, do not mention two-market entry barriers, give little attention to potential entry or maverick firms, and scarcely mention nonprice issues that are often important in vertical relationships. Moreover, they create a safe harbor without a corresponding presumption against vertical mergers involving high-share or dominant firms, and endorse the elimination of double marginalization without adequate caveats.

The current lack of good guidance with respect to vertical mergers has meant that allegations of harm have either been dismissed or require full-blown rule of reason analyses. The latter are invariably complex and costly, and often difficult to convey convincingly to decision-makers.[167] And that, in turn, means that many vertical mergers still do not receive adequate scrutiny and enforcement from the agencies. Given the frequency and importance of such mergers, their ambiguous economic effects, and the weakness of conduct remedies, this record indicates a policy failure that must be reversed.

RECOMMENDATIONS:

(1) *The near per se legality favoring vertical mergers must be explicitly revoked. Guidelines should be issued detailing the nature of and conditions for such competitive concerns as foreclosure, the elimination of potential competition, and the creation of two-market entry barriers.*

(2) *Claims that a vertical merger will eliminate, or is necessary to eliminate, double marginalization must be tested against the alternative of a contract between parties and against other limitations of the theoretical proposition. Claims of other efficiencies and benefits must be assessed by the same standard as for efficiencies generally: past experience or documentation prior to the proposed merger.*

(3) *The agencies must aggressively challenge anticompetitive vertical mergers, continuing to develop arguments and evidence that will be sustained in the courts.*

7.2 Common Ownership

Common ownership—or as it is sometimes called, horizontal shareholding—describes the circumstance in which the major publicly held firms in the same market are at least partially owned and controlled by the same third party or parties. In the most frequently analyzed case, a small number of equity funds hold significant ownership stakes in each of the same few companies in some market, thereby arguably compromising the incentives of those firms to compete against each other. Clearly, in the limit, the logic behind this is unimpeachable: if a single equity fund or other entity holds controlling interests in all firms in a market, that fund would be expected to exercise its control to moderate or eliminate competition among sellers and thereby in-

---

167 A recent example of this is the District Court's opinion in the *AT&T-Time Warner* merger, which contained numerous misunderstandings of economics.

crease industry profits and the value of its combined ownership stake.[168] But where ownership and hence control is less than complete, there remain important conceptual and empirical questions about this scenario. These questions involve the magnitude of the real-world effect when ownership stakes are incomplete, and the mechanism by which it influences firms' operations.

With respect to magnitude, it is clear that institutional shareholding has risen enormously over the past thirty or forty years, now comprising 75 to 80 percent of the stock of all publicly held companies.[169] With that overall increase has come instances of major increases in shareholding by a small number of identical investors in competing companies. Azar et al. report that each of the same five or six major hedge funds and insurance companies hold shares of the stocks of the leading firms in airlines, banking, pharmacies, and tech companies. As shown for airlines, for example, in Table 7.1, these shares can range from 3 or 4 percent at the low end, to 10 percent or more at the upper end.

TABLE 7.1

Largest Institutional Owners in Major Airlines (2016)

American	%	United	%	Southwest	%	Delta	%
T. Rowe Price	13.99	Berkshire Hathaway	9.20	PRIMECAP	11.78	Berkshire Hathaway	8.25
PRIMECAP	8.97	BlackRock	7.11	Berkshire Hathaway	7.02	BlackRock	6.84
Berkshire Hathaway	7.75	Vanguard	6.88	Vanguard	6.21	Vanguard	6.31
Vanguard	6.02	PRIMECAP	6.27	BlackRock	5.96	State Street Global Advisors	4.28
Black Rock	5.82	PAR Capital Mgt.	5.18	Fidelity	5.53	J.P. Morgan Asset Mgt.	3.79
State Street Global Advisors	3.71	State Street Global Advisors	4.28	State Street Global Advisors	3.76	Lansdowne Partners Limited	3.60

Source: Azar et al.

---

168 It is clear that equity funds and other financial interests do influence company's business plans, including at times objecting to "maverick" behavior that diminishes total industry profitability. See, for example, Jeffrey Dustin, JetBlue to charge for checked bags in new airfare class, REUTERS, Nov. 19, 2014.

169 Jose Azar, Martin Schmalz & Isabel Tecu, *Anticompetitive Effects of Common Ownership*, 73 JOURNAL OF FINANCE, 1513-1565 (2018). This increase has been fueled primarily by the growth of pension funds and the rise in index fund investing.

In their work, Azar et al. have reported the first empirical support for an anticompetitive effect from common ownership.[170] In the airline industry, they find that after controlling for other influences, varying degrees of common ownership (and changes therein) of the major carriers are in fact correlated with ticket prices that exceed what otherwise would be expected. Some additional work by the same and other authors have found similar effects in other industries.[171]

This body of work has some critics.[172] They note, for example, the relatively modest extent of actual common shareholding: the total of (say) the same four outside owners of leading firms typically comprises only about 20-25 percent. In addition, the usual index of concentration in shareholding is based on a theoretical model of joint ventures and similar cross-company interests that may lack generality. Furthermore, the estimations have mostly been based on an empirical model of price and concentration that may not be well specified, and in any event does not always seem to yield robust estimates of the magnitude of the effect. This has resulted in some uncertainty about the empirical basis for the common ownership effect.

The other issue that is the subject of debate involves the mechanism through which common shareholding has its effects. As noted previously, it is clear that ultimate owners can and do affect company strategies and decisions, but there is an extensive literature on the principal-agent model that predicts that managerial incentives and actions are nonetheless likely to differ from those of the owners. Studies show this disparity arising even when ownership stakes are larger and more concentrated than in cases cited for common ownership. Where there are multiple common owners whose total shareholdings are not technically controlling and with a majority of shares remaining in the hands of those still interested in single-firm profit maximization, the mechanism by which these multiple minority owners operationalize their stakes would seem to require further explanation. While there are indeed efforts to provide some explanations, as yet it remains unclear which are operative.[173]

---

170 See also Einer Elhauge, *Horizontal Shareholding*, 129 HARVARD LAW REVIEW 5, 1267-1317 (2016).

171 For a good summary, see Matthew Backus, Christopher Conlon & Michael Sinkinso, *The Common Ownership Hypothesis: Theory and Evidence*, BROOKINGS (January 2019).

172 See, for example, Backus et al., *id.* See also Pauline Kennedy, Daniel O'Brien, Minjae Song & Keith Waehrer, *The Competitive Effects of Common Ownership: Economic Foundations and Empirical Evidence*, SSRN: https://ssrn.com/abstract=3008331.

173 See Elhauge, *supra* note 170.

More work is clearly in order. Indeed, that is one conclusion seemingly endorsed by all scholars and policymakers. This is clearly an area deserving of more research and potentially of considerable concern, but at present, there is too much uncertainty to justifiably take policy actions.

RECOMMENDATIONS:

(1) *The exact foundation, magnitude, and effect of common ownership are matters of research importance since its potential effects are not trivial. These should be urgent matters for investigation by the agencies.*

(2) *Specific policy actions should await the findings of research and investigations with respect to common ownership.*

7.3 The Tech Sector and Competition

The rise of the major tech companies and their dominance over important sectors of the economy have raised a number of policy problems, but as noted, our focus here is on their record of mergers and acquisitions. That record is abundant. Over the past twenty or so years, as shown in Table 7.2, the major tech companies—Amazon, Apple, Facebook, Google, and Microsoft—have acquired in total more than 600 companies. Collectively, they have averaged about 25 acquisitions per year between 2005 and 2009, then rising to nearly 50 per year since that time.[174] Google and Microsoft have been the leading acquirers, each with more than 200 acquisitions. Prominent examples include Google's acquisitions of YouTube, Doubleclick, and Waze; Microsoft's acquisitions of LinkedIn and Skype; Facebook's acquisitions of Instagram and WhatsApp; Amazon's acquisitions of IMDb, Audible, and Zappos; and Apple's recent acquisition of Shazam. The targeted companies vary in value from a few hundred thousand dollars in several instances, to the $26 billion that Microsoft paid to acquire LinkedIn and $19 billion paid by Facebook for WhatsApp.

A great many of these 600 acquisitions raise no competitive concerns. Acquisitions of software developers, for example, often target businesses that are unlikely to be able to fully develop and commercialize their innovations by themselves. Other acquisitions result in ease of customer ac-

---

174 List of mergers and acquisitions by Amazon and the other tech companies is taken from Wikipedia, e.g., https://en.wikipedia.org/wiki/List_of_mergers_and_acquisitions_by_Amazon. See also Diana Moss, *The Record of Weak U.S. Merger Enforcement in Big Tech*, American Antitrust Institute, 2019.

cess to seamlessly integrated products. But Moss has reported evidence of weak enforcement in this sector. Specifically, the rate of challenge to mergers in the sector of "data processing, hosting, and related services" —which includes the tech companies—is far lower than the average for all transactions that come before the agencies.[175] Indeed, of the hundreds of acquisitions by the five major tech companies, the FTC and DOJ appear to have challenged exactly one. That one challenge was to Google's planned acquisition of ITA Software, which resulted in its approval subject only to a remedy of questionable effectiveness. And the list of mergers and acquisitions includes some that raise clear competitive concerns.

TABLE 7.2

Total and Major Acquisitions by Leading Tech Companies

Google (200+)	Amazon (80+)	Facebook (50+)	Microsoft (200+)	Apple (70+)
YouTube (2006)	Audible (2008)	Instagram (2012)	LinkedIn (2016)	Shazam (2017)
DoubleClick (2007)	Zappos (2009)	Oculus CR (2014)	Skype (2011)	Akamai (1999 partnership)
ITA (2011)	Whole Foods (2017)	WhatsApp (2014)	Nokia (2013)	
Waze (2013)				
Motorola Mobility (2011)				
Zagat (2011)				
Nest (2014)				

Two distinct types of tech mergers and acquisitions can be identified, one involving target firms that are or might become potential competitors, the other concerning businesses offering goods and services hosted on or complementary to the tech platform. Both of these raise familiar antitrust

---

175 Diana Moss, *The Record of Weak U.S. Merger Enforcement in Big Tech*, American Antitrust Institute, July 2019.

issues—exclusion, innovation, vertical integration, nonprice effects—which become more complicated in the tech sector.

The first concern—where the target company might be a potential rival or substitute—might be viewed as a variation on the previously discussed issue of potential competition. Like all others, the tech companies pay close attention to alternative technologies and services that might displace their current businesses, and so that acquiring a constraining or threatening competitor would seem subject to challenge as such. But the doctrine of potential competition is difficult to apply in ordinary circumstances and is even more difficult to apply in the case of tech companies. One reason for this greater difficulty is that technology in this sector is more fungible and can be adapted to new uses more readily than in traditional goods markets. As a result, identifying a firm that is now not producing a substitute service but might become a potential competitor merely on the basis of some generalized capabilities poses logical—to say nothing of legal—hurdles.

A second reason stems from the dynamism that characterizes the tech sector. Start-up firms may rapidly evolve into viable alternatives to incumbent firms, due to the speed at which consumers may switch and choose their services. Identifying these so-called nascent competitors—small firms that might evolve into real or potential competitors—represents a challenge unlike ordinary goods and services, which must be produced, distributed, and advertised over longer periods of time, and can better be identified as potential alternatives. The result is that an incumbent firm can perceive a nascent threat and acquire that firm before it is more widely apparent that such a firm poses a competitive threat.

These scenarios are illustrated by two important acquisitions by Facebook, first, of Instagram in 2012 and then WhatsApp in 2014. Instagram was a company with few employees and modest revenues that offered a popular photo-sharing app designed for mobile technology where Facebook lagged. Facebook paid $1 billion for Instagram, and the FTC unanimously approved the acquisition. Facebook also offered photo sharing, but the FTC concluded there were numerous other potential rivals, disqualifying Instagram as a uniquely important outside firm. As a possible social media platform, the FTC reportedly did not view Instagram as a competitor to Facebook, although some outside observers recognized the competitive concerns. Contemporaneous news reports noted that Instagram was in fact positioning itself as a social medium[176] and, indeed, a document produced in the FTC

---

176 *Facebook Buys Instagram For $1 Billion, Turns Budding Rival Into Its Standalone Photo App*, TECHCRUNCH, April 2012.

investigation quoted a high-ranking Facebook executive explaining that the Instagram purchase was to eliminate a potential competitor.[177] The trade press at the time even declared that the purpose of the acquisition was simply to "scoop up what could have eventually become a big rival."[178]

Two years later the FTC also approved Facebook's $19 billion acquisition of WhatsApp, a messaging service popular outside the U.S. While little is public about the reasons for FTC approval, the parallel EU investigation may provide some insight. It concluded that WhatsApp's real-time messaging and Facebook's social networking posting service were distinct, so there was no competitive overlap. Documents later released showed, however, that Facebook had been following WhatsApp for some time and viewed it "not just as a rising competitor but as a potential Facebook killer."[179]

These two acquisitions suggest both the difficulty of identifying a firm with potential or nascent properties but also the failure of policy to weigh certain competitive concerns sufficiently seriously. These tensions have been on full display in other cases involving the tech sector. Google's 2007 acquisition of DoubleClick combined Google's massive ad sales operation with DoubleClick's key ad placement services. Both companies had explored or begun development of technologies capable of invading the other's core business. The FTC majority nonetheless approved the merger, dismissing the importance of Google as an entrant into ad servicing by asserting that Google was not "uniquely positioned to have a substantial competition-enhancing effect."[180] It also rejected the concern that the combined company might engage in various anticompetitive actions with the argument that DoubleClick itself did not have market power and that leveraging theories were undermined by the ease with which customers could switch to alternatives.

A dissenting statement of one FTC Commissioner at the time expressed unease with this dismissal of competitive concerns, noting among other things that Google's enormous resources ensured completion of development

---

177 Josh Kosman, *Facebook Boasted of Buying Instagram to Kill the Competition*, NEW YORK POST, Feb. 26, 2019. The prices paid by Facebook for Instagram and WhatsApp seem to exceed—perhaps to an enormous degree—the obvious value of the target companies, suggesting that the motivation behind the acquisitions was more to eliminate a potential rival than to achieve some type of efficiencies.

178 Adrian Covert, *Facebook Buys WhatsApp for $19 Billion*, CNN TECH, Feb. 19, 2014.

179 "These Confidential Charts Show Why Facebook Acquired WhatsApp," Buzzfeed, December 2018.

180 Statement, U.S. Federal Trade Commission, Statement of the Federal Trade Commission Concerning Google/DoubleClick (December 2007).

of its own ad servicing program and that the merger would result in the termination of that project as well as entry by DoubleClick into ad intermediation that would potentially compete with Google.[181] This dissent proved more accurate than the FTC majority's views. Recent accounts indicate that Google has tied together products in anticompetitive ways, become the unavoidable source for ad intermediation, and driven out major possible competitors.[182]

These cases demonstrate the limitations of current policy and standards. Even when the antitrust agency can envision how one technology might evolve into a potential competitor to the tech company, it lacks any reliable way of assessing the probability that might happen. In other cases, the possibility of a competitive technology may rest with a start-up firm whose capabilities are unclear to almost all observers, including perhaps the firm itself. But if "likelihood" is the obstacle to enforcement actions against such mergers, then the standard for prohibiting mergers in the tech sector may need to be adjusted to match the likely available evidence and indications. For example, the criteria for challenging a potential competition merger could be stated as prohibiting the acquisition of any firm with a technology that is sufficiently fungible that it might plausibly be adapted to challenge the products and services offered by the tech company. This criterion might be coupled with a stipulation that there be no defense due to ease of entry or claims of efficiencies.

A different, but equally difficult, set of problems relates to the competitive issues arising from tech companies acquiring businesses to be hosted on or complementary to their own platforms. By virtue of their dominance, a tech company's acquisitions can result in a number of competitive problems. These include steering customers to its own acquired business, disadvantaging possible rivals and start-ups through network effects, creating or enhancing barriers to new entry, reducing consumer choice, slowing innovation, and over time virtually requiring new businesses to subscribe to the dominant platform, where, of course, they also become subject to platform strategies that may work to their disadvantage.[183] These possible scenarios

---

181 Statement, U.S. Federal Trade Commission, Dissenting Statement of Commissioner Pamela Jones Harbour (December 2007). Indeed, whatever the premerger entry barriers, they were surely increased by agency approval of the merger since any possible entrant would now be facing DoubleClick wedded to Google.

182 Keach Hagey & Vivien Ngo, *How Google Edged Out Rivals and Built the World's Dominant Ad Machine*, WALL STREET JOURNAL, Nov. 7, 2019.

183 For further discussion, see Jean Tirole, "A Nobel Prize-Winning Economist's Guide to Taming Tech Monopolies." Also, Carl Shapiro, *Protecting Competition in the American Economy: Merger Control, Tech Titans, and Labor Markets*, 33 JOURNAL OF ECONOMIC PERSPECTIVES 3, 69-63, (2019).

are commonly illustrated by Google's acquisition of Waze, Microsoft's acquisition of Skype, and Amazon's acquisition of Zappos, among many others.

The need to be on a particular platform may permit that platform monopoly to impose conditions on the hosted company's operation that ensure it is not too strong a competitor to the tech company itself. Amazon seeks, for example, to prevent hosted products from offering products at lower prices through other distribution channels, and now has begun selling its own branded products using some data from third-party sellers on its site.[184] Moreover, it uses information about the success of some hosted products and services to guide its own competitive initiatives, which in turn undermine start-ups. These actions serve both to exploit its dominant position and to insulate it from competition by others.

Google has similarly engaged in a variety of conduct that alters search so as to increase its sales of advertising. The EU has been vigorous in addressing these practices, alleging that "when a consumer enters a query into the Google search engine…Google's comparison shopping service…results…are displayed at or near the top" and that it has demoted rivals through the use of algorithms that systematically skew results in its favor.[185] Google has for years also been altering the appearance of text ads in its search results in ways that increasingly blur the lines between the two. The most recent change has resulted in such subtle differences that search users have inadvertently clicked on paid ads, potentially distorting consumer choice but increasing Google's ad revenues.[186]

In these and other ways, the necessity of being on these platforms leads inexorably to subtle disadvantages being imposed on hosted companies. For platforms that involve search and choice, such as Amazon and Google, behavioral considerations result in consumer deference to choices presented first, or more prominently, or as defaults, thereby creating impediments to other competitors. These impediments can be reinforced by methods used by the hosting platforms to rank and place alternatives. Algorithms used for such purposes are inherently a combination of objective and judgmental factors, with incentives inevitably playing a role and with their invisibility preventing effective policy review. In recent years all of these factors have contributed to diminishing prospects for tech start-ups. Indeed, venture

---

184 Nandita Bose & Jeffrey Dustin, *Amazon Admits It Uses Aggregated Seller Data to Help Business*, REUTERS, Nov. 13, 2019.

185 European Commission, "Commission fines Google $2.4 billion euros for abusing dominance as search engine by giving illegal advantage to own comparison shopping service," Brussels, June 2017.

186 "Google Tries a New Look. Users Balk," NEW YORK TIMES, Jan. 31, 2020.

capital to developers whose products and services directly confront the major tech companies has reportedly been in sharp decline.[187]

Antitrust has generally been slow to recognize the long-term harm to competition from these practices. Attempts to use rules and fines to prevent a variety of anticompetitive practices have not had their full intended effect. The EU, for example, has been engaged with Google on its shopping services for years, striving repeatedly to fashion rules that would level the playing field for other players and for the benefit of consumers. Even substantial fines have not resolved the competitive issues. The reasons for these failures are very much the same as those associated with conduct-type remedies to mergers, as was discussed in Chapter 6. Like those remedies, the use of rules in an effort to control certain profit-increasing but anticompetitive actions by the tech companies are difficult to write due to the large number of contingencies that need to be allowed for, and the many ways in which those companies' technologies permit them to evade the intent of the rules. Violations are often difficult to observe and subject to pretextual explanations—some of which may, of course, be legitimate, but no less difficult to assess. The antitrust agencies that set out these rules are ill equipped to oversee them or take prompt and effective action against violations. And when violations do become apparent, often those simply prompt rewrites of the rules or new rules that attempt to catch up with firms' evasive strategies, in a continuing cat-and-mouse game, with antitrust constantly one step behind.

The inadequacy of traditional methods of preventing the anticompetitive consequences of acquisitions of complementors again suggests the need for a broader, and perhaps blunter, policy. One possible policy would involve a broad mandate for interoperability, requiring the dominant platforms to provide access to their platforms and to the underlying data. Similar to what has been done in the case of British open banking regulations, this would facilitate entry of services on the core platform business. A second possible policy would limit or ban a dominant platform from any acquisition that distorts that platform's own incentives. This policy would address the incentive issue associated with hosted services, but of course would prompt controversy about what represented a prohibited line of business.

One step further down this path would be to designate certain platforms as utilities that are simply prohibited from mergers and acquisitions.

---

187 "Prime Leverage: A Retail Giant's Hold on Tech," NEW YORK TIMES, Dec. 16, 2019. Venture capital has reportedly shrunk by 90 percent for those developers and instead has shifted to less directly competing ventures. Steve Lohr & Erin Griffith, *With Big Tech in Their Paths, Start-Ups Turn to Business Markets*, NEW YORK TIMES, Nov. 22, 2019.

This would be consistent with some policies in the telecom and electricity sectors that have sought to prevent platform owners from commercial operation on their own platform. While such restrictions might well result in some inefficiencies, that argument should not automatically prevail against the benefits of openness of the market.

As this discussion has shown, current tools for merger control are not well suited to these unconventional settings. Rather, new and unconventional antitrust measures would seem necessary. As noted, these may well involve outright prohibitions on certain mergers and acquisitions. They may also require unwinding some past mergers and acquisitions that have proven especially harmful and represent enduring obstacles to competition.[188] While dissolution of companies is difficult, there is no reason that it should not be considered as a policy tool under current circumstances in the tech sector.

Finally, consideration should be given to the creation of a digital competition agency, one with resident expertise in the tech sector and with regulatory powers to complement those of the antitrust agencies with respect to considerations that are distinct to the tech sector. Such an institution would also be able to intervene more quickly than the antitrust agency and to establish regulations to complement any conventional antitrust actions by the agencies to protect competition in the tech sector.

RECOMMENDATIONS:

(1) Because network effects confer lasting advantage, the dominant tech and platform companies should bear the burden of proof to demonstrate that any mergers and acquisitions have demonstrable procompetitive effects.

(2) Where there is any likelihood that a target company's technology might evolve or can be modified to challenge any part of a dominant tech company, an acquisition should be per se illegal. There should be no need for proof that the nascent competitor's business model presently includes such a strategy and no defense due to claims of easy entry or efficiencies.

---

188 To be clear, this recommendation does not apply to the platform itself. Attempts to break up Google or Amazon would not likely result in lasting fragmentation due to network effects and first mover advantages favoring the dominant incumbent. The break-ups should focus on potential competitors and hosted firms and services.

(3) Consideration should be given to a moratorium on all mergers and acquisitions by the large tech companies in order to allow the agencies to develop better methods for analysis. The moratorium period should also be used to launch a specialized digital competition regulator.

(4) The use of rules to limit pricing or other terms and conditions that disadvantage hosted independent applications on tech platforms must not be relied upon. Similar to rule-based conduct remedies, these are easier to avoid than to write, and often unenforceable. Structural solutions—for example, preventing a tech company from having a financial interest in any hosted application or site—should be considered instead.

(5) Consideration should be given to dissolving past tech sector mergers when the basis for their approval has proven erroneous and when the merger has instead entrenched and extended the tech company's dominance.

REFORMING THE MERGER CONTROL PROCESS: Retrospectives, Resources, and the Judiciary

The substantive reforms outlined in the preceding chapters represent the core of a revived merger control policy that would go far toward remedying errors and weaknesses of past practice. They would not, however, be entirely sufficient since policy reforms do not arise and become effective in a vacuum. Implementing these reforms in fact requires resolving several impediments to sound policy process. Primary among these are the greater use of retrospective evaluations, increases in agency resources, and strengthening judicial education. Indeed, without addressing these process issues, some of the necessary substantive reforms would be at a minimum slowed or altogether jeopardized. Greater scrutiny of mergers or more challenges, for example, will not be possible without the resources to follow through. An unreceptive judiciary will render efforts to restore and extend enforcement moot. And the failure to exploit and learn from past experience will unnecessarily delay improvements.

This section sets out recommendations for improving the merger control process and thereby ensuring an effective as well as comprehensive program of merger reforms. In each case we detail the rationale for and specifics of the necessary reforms.

8.1 Retrospectives on Mergers and Enforcement

There is no dispute that over time merger control has undergone substantial changes and improvements. These have drawn on theoretical advances (for example, upward pricing pressure), empirically based insights (ostensibly, the HHI thresholds), and general economics (e.g., criteria for efficiencies). But there is one large—and largely untapped—source of insights for improving merger control, namely, actual experience with enforcement practice by the agencies. The agencies' history of choices of mergers to investigate, methods of analysis, determinations made, and ultimate resolutions of these matters represents a body of arguably the most relevant experience from which to learn. Paired with measures of outcomes and good techniques for assessment, this history has enormous potential to improve understanding of policies and their effects.

One clear demonstration of the value is, ironically, from agency experience itself. In the 1990s, after losing several challenges to hospital mergers, the FTC suspended legal challenges and instead launched a series of economic studies of prior hospital mergers in order to be better able to demonstrate their competitive harm. This initiative produced several high-quality studies demonstrating the harmful consequences of such mergers as well as identifying certain weaknesses in the agency's approach to challenging them. These merger retrospectives[189] proved to be important in renewed and successful efforts to challenge additional hospital mergers. It is surprising that, despite this demonstration of their value, the FTC has not followed up with a program of initiatives in systematic program of retrospectives for mergers in other industries or for other competitive concerns.[190]

This experience underscores another point, namely, that the FTC and DOJ are best able to conduct these studies due to the data and other information that they gather as a by-product of merger enforcement. Outside researchers, by contrast, lack access to information about particular companies and cases and hence cannot easily conduct the same type of retrospectives. Without access to such data, academic work on *ex post* evaluation has unfolded at a relatively slow pace.

That said, over time published merger retrospectives by academics have cumulated into a substantial enough number to allow for compilation

---

189 Merger retrospectives can take several forms but the most common is so-called "difference-in-differences." This first measures the change in price (or some other outcome variable) before and after a merger, and then controls for other influences such as cost changes by netting out the price change that occurred at the same time for an otherwise similar product not affected by the merger. For example, an airline merger might be found to increase price on some route served by the merging carriers. The effect of fuel price changes and other non-merger influences could be netted out by measuring the price change on similar other routes not affected by the merger. For further discussion of this technique and its technical requirements, see John Kwoka, *MMCR* (2015).

190 As already noted, the FTC did conduct evaluations of its remedy policy, and their economics staff have periodically undertaken several merger retrospectives, but these represent episodic efforts. The Justice Department has altogether fewer initiatives in this area.

and analysis of their collective implications. My research monograph is precisely this exercise, and its implications provide further confirmation of the value of retrospective evaluations of mergers. *MMCR* compiled all qualifying published merger retrospectives into a common format that permitted a so-called "meta-analysis."[191] *MMCR* included about 60 individually studied mergers and another 3000 or so that were studied at a more aggregated level. It came to a number of notable findings, some of which have already been cited. Prominent among these have been the fact that merger enforcement has substantially narrowed its focus over time, that increases in price followed from most mergers, and that merger remedies (and especially conduct remedies) have often proven ineffective. The significance of these results underscores the potential of merger retrospectives to inform and improve policy.

These experiences with merger retrospectives highlight three quite different possible purposes that they can serve. At one extreme, a retrospective performed on an individual merger can help understand the outcome of policy in the case of a particularly important merger—important perhaps due to its size or its controversial nature.[192] Alternatively, a group of retrospectives targeting a particular industry or issue—such as those in the FTC's hospital initiative—serve to develop a body of evidence helpful in understanding a specific enforcement matter. And finally, a large data base of merger retrospectives in numerous industries casts light on the question of whether merger enforcement overall is in fact addressing the "right" mergers, or too many, or too few.

There is merit to all of these, and there have long been calls for more retrospectives. Carlton[193] was among the first to note the lack of merger policy evaluations and set out some methodological considerations for how they should be performed. Kovacic seconded this, urging "greater attention to the evaluation of the economic effects of enforcement decisions."[194] An OECD

---

191 Mergers, Merger Control, and Remedies, op. cit. A meta-analysis aggregates and summarizes multiple studies of some issue. It has some criteria for inclusion of studies and combines their results in the search for common findings and other implications. This technique increases sample size and provides stronger evidence than that from a single or a few such studies.

192 For example, see Orley Ashenfeler, Daniel Hoskens & Matthew Weinberg, *Price Effects of a Large Manufacturing Merger: A Case Study of Maytag-Whirlpool,* 5 AMERICAN ECONOMIC JOURNAL: ECONOMIC POLICY 2013, 1, 239–261 (2013).

193 Dennis Carlton, *Why We Need to Measure the Effect of Merger Policy and How to Do It,* 5 COMPETITION POLICY INTERNATIONAL (2009).

194 William Kovacic, *Assessing the Quality of Competition Policy: The Case of Horizontal Merger Enforcement,* 5 COMPETITION POLICY INTERNATIONAL (2009).

roundtable and report have recommended the same,[195] as have Jarsulic & myself[196] and, now, many others. Moreover, competition agencies in some other countries now conduct impact evaluations of their merger policy on a regular basis, and increasing consideration is being given to doing so at the FTC and Justice Department, although as yet no such program has been launched.[197]

To be sure, conducting any retrospectives raises methodological and resource issues. Methodologically, there are questions as to which and how many mergers to evaluate, the choice and measurement of outcomes, and the exact form of empirical testing. There are issues of resources that can be devoted to assessing past mergers as opposed to current enforcement actions by the agencies. Without discounting these realities, there are some countervailing factors to be considered.

With respect to resources, it is important to realize that conducting retrospectives is an investment in improving future enforcement policy since by conducting such studies, the agencies would develop insights into how to make on-going merger policy both more efficient as well as more effective. It would do so by providing guidance regarding characteristics of competitively problematic mergers, choices made by the agencies with respect to challenges, and strategies to ensure effective resolution and remedies of these. For this reason, Farrell & I have described this resource saving argument as a "false economy."[198]

In fact, it is not clear that the resource burden of conducting merger retrospectives is always so great. The usual methodology of merger retrospectives—difference-in-differences—typically requires only a modest amount of data and could be undertaken by the antitrust agencies on a regular basis.[199] For some industries such as domestic airlines, the necessary data are readily available from the Department of Transportation. But more generally, at

---

195 OECD Roundtable, *Impact Evaluation of Merger Decisions* (2014), http://www. oecd.org/daf/competition/Impactevaluationofmergerdecisions2011.pdf.

196 *MMCR*. See also Marc Jarsulic & John Kwoka, *Evidence-Based Policy in Antitrust: The Need for Ongoing Merger Retrospectives,* PROMARKET (2017), https:// promarket.org/evidence-based-policy-antitrust-need-ongoing-merger-retrospectives/.

197 Notably, the UK Competition and Markets Commission is required to perform *ex post* evaluations of at least two cases each year. In the U.S., The 21st Century Competition Commission Act (H.R. 4686) was introduced in the House of Representatives in 2017, requiring the agencies to undertake a small number of retrospectives each year.

198 Joseph Farrell & John Kwoka, *Resetting Merger Policy in the New Administration,* 4 CONCURRENCES (2016).

199 See *MMCR* for discussion of certain additional econometric issues.

least some of the data requirements could be alleviated by mandating that all merging parties produce the necessary post-merger data as a condition of merger settlements or even of the initial HSR filing. This would be justified by the benefit of having the agencies better able to assess the results of their decisions and policies with respect to proposed mergers.

It should also be noted that FTC staff in fact do conduct a small number of merger retrospectives on an on-going basis. Some of these retrospectives focus on their own past cases, while in other instances the reason for the choice is less clear. But since the agency is conducting some number of retrospectives anyway, it is clearly the case that some resources for conducting retrospectives do exist, and it follows that the FTC can deploy these to choose which mergers are to be evaluated. The DOJ currently lacks the same data-gathering authority as the FTC, but that does not prevent some retrospectives from being undertaken. Moreover, if necessary, similar authority could be granted to DOJ.

Of course, not all cases can be studied, raising the issue of which cases the agency should choose. If that decision is left entirely to the agency, it would run some risk that cases might appear to be selected—or actually be selected—to confirm the best of the agency' decisions, or its most innocuous errors, instead of truly informative cases. One method to check on this would be to have the agency's choice subject to approval by a neutral outside entity, perhaps the chief economist at the GAO or some outside expert panel. These issues can and should be resolved as part of a strengthened program of merger evaluations.

RECOMMENDATIONS:

> (1) The agencies need to initiate programs of ex post evaluations of some number of mergers each year. Available resources should be redeployed and additional resources should be provided for these programs. DOJ should be granted data-gathering authority comparable to that of the FTC for these purposes.

> (2) Agencies need to develop specific purposes for their programs of mergers to be evaluated—to cast light on especially important cases, or to evaluate a particular industry or issue, or to assess overall merger policy. Agencies' programs and choices should be overseen by a neutral party to ensure optimal targeting.

> (3) As a condition of their filing and investigation by the agencies, merging companies should be required to produce post-merger data necessary to conduct evaluations of the outcomes.

8.2 Agency Resources

The two antitrust agencies—the Federal Trade Commission and the Antitrust Division of the Justice Department—share responsibilities for merger control and other antitrust issues. Although the scope of their tasks has expanded over time—and is certain to expand further in the face of growing needs—increases in their budgets have not kept up with the resource requirements to fully perform those tasks.[200] Accordingly, one essential component of merger reforms is an increase in their resources in order to ensure their capacity to effectively pursue their mission.

The need for additional resources is readily apparent from an examination of the sheer number of reported mergers. Most mergers over a certain size—currently about $90 million—must be pre-notified to the antitrust agencies. Since the agencies give at least cursory review of all the reported mergers to determine which to formally investigate, the number of reported mergers is at least a rough measure of the demands imposed on the agency by outside events. The data in Table 8.1 shows a dramatic rise in those numbers between 2010 and 2018. In that period, the number of reported mergers nearly tripled, rising from 716 to 2111. Since the year 2010 may have been a bit of an anomaly due to the financial crisis, one could justifiably compare 2011 to 2018. But even then, the number of mergers nearly doubled, from 1166 to 2111. Clearly there has been a major merger wave over the past decade.

The next question is how have agency budgets responded. To be sure, agency budgets cover non-merger matters as well as mergers, and in addition, budgets change with a lag. For those reasons, agency budgets might not be expected to double or triple over this period, but there nonetheless should be a measurable increase in order to permit scrutiny and investigations of the rising number of competitively problematic mergers.[201] Table 8.1 documents the antitrust budgets for the DOJ and the FTC during the 2000-2018 period. As shown there, the increases in nominal budgets are minuscule for DOJ and modest for the FTC—1.1 percent and 11.2 percent,

---

200 Indeed, certain of the recommendations herein would at least initially enlarge the mission of the agencies and require additional resources—pursuit of potential competition mergers, for example. On the other hand, once fully established, greater reliance on the structural presumption would help reduce their burden.

201 The implicit assumption is that some roughly constant fraction of reported mergers deserve scrutiny. If anything, it seems more likely that as the merger wave has grown, an ever-larger fraction of mergers test enforcement boundaries, reinforcing these conclusions.

respectively, over nine years. In inflation-adjusted terms,[202] both have in fact declined—by 10.1 percent for DOJ and by 3.7 percent for the FTC. The total of both agency antitrust budgets has fallen by 8.0 percent in real terms over this period, even as the number of mergers has increased dramatically.

Compounding matters, agency budgets have become more constraining over time due to the rising costs of merger investigations. These costs have risen for several reasons. One is the diminished role for the structural presumption. A presumption against certain mergers would minimize the legal and economic burden on the agencies, whereas at present essentially all potentially problematic mergers, regardless of size, undergo full and expensive evaluation. The economic methodology for evaluating mergers has become increasingly complex, laden with sophisticated concepts and often requiring substantial amounts of company data, sophisticated economic modeling and econometric analysis, and vigorous (and expensive) disputes between the agencies and the merging parties. Hiring and retaining the necessary talent, especially in competition with defendant law firms and economic consultancies, is an ever more costly proposition. For all of these reasons, estimates of the costs of bringing a major case run into the tens of millions of dollars for the agencies, and yet more for deep-pocketed merging parties.

The predictable effect of sharply rising demands, rising costs, and flat or even declining resources is relatively fewer investigations or less thorough scrutiny of mergers. While thoroughness is difficult to measure, the data confirms this effect on the scope of enforcement. Table 8.1 reports that the total number of merger investigations conducted by the two agencies has risen between 2010 and 2017, but only from 42 to 45. Indeed, the 45 investigations conducted in 2018 is the lowest number since 2010, in the aftermath of the financial crisis when total merger numbers were a fraction of the current level.

The implication of these data is that the agencies' current capacity for merger enforcement appears to be roughly about 45 to 50 investigations per year. Additional mergers are simply less likely to get the scrutiny they deserve since the agencies lack the necessary resources. But with rising numbers of reported mergers, this capacity constraint suggests a declining intensity of enforcement over time. This is indeed the case. Table 8.1 shows—and Figure 8.2 illustrates—that in 2010-2011 about 3.8 or 3.9 percent of reported mergers were investigated, but that percentage has been falling ever since. In the following three years the percent dropped to a range of about 3.2 to 3.6

---

202 The GDP Price Index rose by 14.9 percent during this period.

percent, and in the latest three-year period it is down to 2.1 to 3.0 percent. Using the first and last three-year averages, mergers in the latest period of time are about 30 percent less likely even to be investigated than in the earlier period.

TABLE 8.1

Merger Investigations and Agency Funding
FTC and DOJ, 2010-2018

YEAR	ANTITRUST FUNDING				MERGERS AND INVESTIGATIONS		
	ANTITRUST DIVISION FUNDING ($M)	FTC COMPETITION FUNDING ($M)	TOTAL FUNDING ($M)	TOTAL FUNDING ($M DEFLATED)	MERGERS REPORTED UNDER HSR	NUMBER INVESTI-GATED	PERCENT INVESTI-GATED
2010	163.2	125.1	288.3	288.3	716	42	3.8
2011	162.8	125.3	288.1	282.2	1166	55	3.9
2012	159.6	135.8	295.4	284.0	1429	49	3.5
2013	159.0	135.9	294.9	278.7	1326	47	3.6
2014	160.2	129.5	289.7	271.3	1663	51	3.2
2015	162.2	127.1	289.3	268.4	1801	47	2.6
2016	165.0	135.7	300.7	274.1	1832	54	3.0
2017	165.0	134.2	299.2	266.9	2052	51	2.6
2018	165.0	139.7	304.7	265.2	2111	45	2.1

Note: Percent investigated is calculated based on a total adjusted for timing of reports and investigations.

Source: HSR Annual Report, DOJ and FTC, 2018; Federal Trade Commission Fiscal Years 2010-2018 Congressional Budget Justification.

FIGURE 8.1

Number of Reported Mergers (left scale)
and Total Antitrust Agency Funding (right scale)

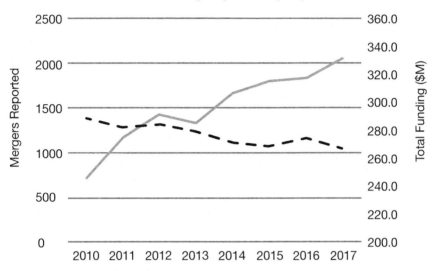

FIGURE 8.2

Percent of Reported Mergers Subject to Investigation

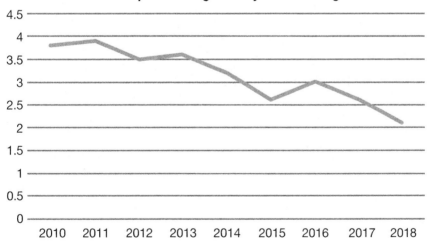

Given that the mission of the agencies is to police a $20 trillion economy, with 1500-2000 sizeable mergers per year, and with little or no increase to antitrust agency budgets, it is not surprising that the resource constraint binds, and binds ever more tightly with each passing year. The result is that the antitrust mission suffers at a time where its role should be expanding. These considerations argue for a greater resource base for the antitrust agencies. Proposals for increases in agency resources, however, immediately run up against an unfavorable national budgetary climate. There are, however, two straightforward policy changes that would offer some relief to agency budgets. Parties to prospective mergers must file preliminary documents with the agencies and simultaneously pay a filing fee. These fees, currently nominal, could be significantly increased to match the rising costs of merger investigations. Beyond that, at present these fees do not expand agency budgets but rather serve to offset congressional appropriations as sources of funds for the agency budgets. The current fee structure involves a maximum filing fee of $280,000 for any proposed acquisition of $940,000,000 or more in assets. A more reasonable fee structure would be .05 or .06 percent—that is, .0005 or .0006—of the acquired firm's assets. That would effectively double the current filing for a proposed acquisition of billion dollars, but would quite sensibly rise for any larger acquisition.[203] The second important policy change would therefore allow those fees to flow directly into agency budgets.[204] Among other virtues of this approach, this method would serve to better match agency resources to current workload.

Because workload varies considerably over time, it might also be prudent to allow the agencies to smooth their fee-based resources by banking unused resources over some very limited period of time, perhaps one to two years. This would avoid a "use it or lose it" property to the fees but may require some oversight to ensure proper use of this discretion. This might include, at a minimum, explanations for any year-to-year resource transfers, but it would certainly increase the ability of the agencies to mobilize the resources as necessary to address the irregular pattern of tasks they face.

Resources, of course, are necessary but not sufficient for improving agency effectiveness. Of singular importance is dedication of the agency leadership to good policy and practice, and motivation of staff to do the same. This has not always been the case, with agencies at times seeming

---

203 These numbers are consistent with amounts proposed in the Antitrust Enforcement
Improvements Act of 2019. In some other agencies, filing fees do in fact result in direct
increases in agency budgets.

204 In some other agencies, such filing fees do indeed flow to agency budgets. There are current legislative proposals to raise these fees for mergers and to have them automatically increase antitrust agency budgets.

determined to avoid litigation and instead to find reasons to approve mergers that appear transparently anticompetitive. Greater resources must be paired with a commitment to the agency mission.

RECOMMENDATIONS:

> *(1) Resources at the FTC and DOJ for antitrust purposes, and for merger evaluation in particular, must be increased. Merger filing fees should be raised to reflect the substantial costs of investigations, especially of large mergers, and should flow directly into increases in agency budgets.*

> *(2) The agencies need to seek methods for conserving on resources needing to be allocated to merger control, such as greater reliance on presumptions and more extensive use of retrospectives.*

8.3 Judicial Education in Modern Merger Analysis

Much of the reform program just described would operate at the agency level, but for it ultimately to be truly effective, the judiciary must be equipped to understand and apply modern merger analysis in appeals that almost inevitably come before it.[205] Federal district court judges hearing merger cases must be able, for example, to grasp the foundation of the Merger Guidelines—market substitution and definition, methods for determining competitive harms, the role of measured concentration, standards for evidence and proof—as well as basic economic concepts such as incentives, bargaining, diversion, and so forth.[206] They must also be receptive to arguments concerning potential competition, exclusionary practices, innovation issues, barriers to entry, and other competitive concerns.

Concern for their ability to convey such technical issues to the courts alters the behavior of the antitrust agencies. It almost certainly leads to agency reluctance to bringing certain challenges where the economic arguments might be subtle and instead settle cases through remedies (and weak ones at that), rather than expending resources on trials that risk achieving even less. Indeed, a constant fear is "making bad law," that is, not just losing

---

205 The terms "modern merger analysis" and "modern antitrust" are sometimes still used to describe the now thirty-year old Chicago attack on fifty-year-old antitrust, despite both being well out of date.

206 The Justice Department has made this very point in its recent appeal of a federal district court's decision to permit the merger of AT&T and Time Warner to proceed. See Motion of the United States, U.S. Dep't of Justice, May 2018. Full disclosure: I consulted for the Justice Department in this case.

the case at hand but having a judicial opinion so adverse that it complicates similar future cases. The result is that the agencies on balance challenge too few mergers—focusing on securing wins rather than bringing all cases that should be brought, much less using the law to its limits in challenging anticompetitive mergers. The proof of this is, ironically, that the agencies often proudly proclaim their very high winning record as indicative of their effectiveness. In reality, a perfect winning record is the clearest possible indicator that the agency is not pursuing all the cases it should, but rather, limiting its case-bringing to those with safe and predictably successful outcomes.[207]

The challenge represented by the courts has multiple sources. One factor is that antitrust trials are infrequent, so that a federal district court judge might see a merger case only once every five or ten years. This creates a burden on the court to get up to speed in a specialized area of the law that is unlike any other—a challenge that is often not met. The result has too often been judicial opinions that seem uninformed or erratic, with distressing implications for agency enforcement choices and for antitrust policy more generally. Alternatives such as specialized antitrust courts have sometimes been recommended, but a simpler reform would be to have antitrust trials be heard by three-judge panels rather than by a single judge. This would increase the likelihood of bringing relevant experience into the proceeding and reduce the variability of outcomes and opinions by a single adjudicator.

Another complicating factor is the Chicago school *laissez-faire* view of mergers and many business practices that has become deeply seated in the judiciary. Despite being discredited,[208] this view has created a hard tilt against antitrust intervention and in favor of efficiency explanations for myriad practices and mergers. Most recently, as already discussed, this has been evidenced by the movement to elevate so-called Type I errors—the risk of disallowing an efficient merger or practice—as the critical sin of antitrust. As noted before, what evidence there is suggests that Type II errors—failing to prevent anticompetitive mergers and actions—are a greater risk and with greater costs, but this has not prevented appeals to Type I errors as a nearly sufficient reason to decide against the agencies.

---

207 A further reason why won-loss records are misleading indicators of agency impact is that they cannot take account of any deterrence effects of mergers.

208 For a thorough analysis, see Jonathan Baker, *Taking the Error Out of 'Error Cost' Analysis: What's Wrong with Antitrust's Right*, 80 ANTITRUST LAW JOURNAL 1, (2015). It is ironic that even as these simplistic free market views have been in retreat in economics, they have become ever more entrenched in the judiciary.

Over the past forty years or so, the Chicago view has been sustained and expanded by its active promotion by think tanks, centers, and university programs funded by big business and private donors committed to *laissez-faire* policies. Among the most shrewdly targeted of these is the so-called "judicial education" program of the Law and Economics Center ("LEC") hosted at George Mason University and funded by major corporate interests.[209] This program proudly announces that "[t]o date, over 5,000 federal and state judges from all 50 states and the District of Columbia, including three current U.S. Supreme Court Justices, have participated in at least one of the LEC's judicial education programs."[210] There is nothing remotely equivalent that provides judges with an alternative mainstream, much less progressive perspective on antitrust economics and policy.

Progress in instituting real and necessary reforms of merger policy will therefore require a judicial education program to counterbalance the outdated but heavily entrenched Chicago school view. It will also require a dedicated and consistent effort by the agencies—and by agency leadership—to present the courts with clear and cogent arguments, buttressed by the best possible evidence, for the policies described herein. While this risks losing the occasional case, it would become part of a concerted effort to establish sound arguments against certain mergers and practices, and would represent a signal to companies of the agencies' determination to challenge them. Such an effort by the agencies would in the longer-term help to rebalance the judiciary's current tilt away from sound antitrust principles and practice.

RECOMMENDATIONS:

(1) Judicial education in modern mainstream merger analysis is needed in order to ensure decisions reflecting current understanding and standards.

(2) The creation of three-judge panels to hear antitrust proceedings would help improve the quality and consistency of the outcomes of litigation.

---

209 The Center for Public Integrity, *Corporations, Pro-Business Nonprofits Foot Bill for Judicial Seminars*, www.publicintegrity.org/2013/03/28/12368/corporations-pro-business-nonprofits-foot-bill-judicial-seminars.

210 Mason Judicial Education Program, https://masonlec.org/divisions/mason-judicial-education-program/.

CHAPTER 9

Controlling Mergers:
A Summing Up

This book began with the proposition that merger control in the U.S. suffers from a number of distinct weaknesses that have resulted in a much too permissive policy. We have identified no fewer than fifteen areas requiring significant reforms, covering virtually all aspects of merger policy. The sheer number underscores how vast has been the gap between current policy and what is required in order to protect competition. But this research is ultimately not about documenting the various flaws and errors of policy, but rather a compendium of specific recommendations for strengthening merger control policy. They cover the proper role of market structure, methods for dealing with efficiencies and entry, and the effects from potential competition, nonprice issues, and monopsony. In addition, they address remedies, vertical mergers, common ownership, and the tech sector. And finally, attention is paid to the need for merger retrospectives, agency resources, and judicial education.

For each of these topic areas, we have provided background to the issue followed by economic evidence for how it can be addressed. This has resulted in a comprehensive set of specific recommendations, some 44 in all, covering the full range of substantive issues in current merger policy and practice needing reform. They rely on the best evidence and the most appropriate economic modeling. Implementing them would strengthen the economic and administrative foundations of policy. It would make the enforcement process more certain and more consistent. It would simplify the enforcement process and make it more efficient. It would not so much expand merger control policy as it would restore the original meaning of the term "competition" as the antitrust agencies' mission.

Most of the substantive reform proposals, it should be noted, could be implemented unilaterally by the agencies. The agencies do not need further legislative authority, for example, to enforce current guidelines or to rely on the structural presumption; to pay greater attention to nonprice effects, innovation, and impediments to entry; and to more firmly resist arguments with respect to efficiencies and avoid the use of remedies. These are all within their legal authority, and indeed, arguably already their responsibility, a responsibility that has not always been met in practice.

A few other reforms might require minor modifications of legislative authority or at least formal agency guidance. For example, challenges to potential competition mergers would be facilitated by legislative language that stated that mergers eliminating a potential entrant should be evaluated using the same standard of proof as all others. A more aggressive stance toward vertical mergers would be facilitated by the issuance of sound vertical merger guidelines that set out conditions for likely violations in terms of foreclosure, two-market entry, and other well-known harms to competition. And all of these reforms would require resources for the agency commensurate with the tasks required of them.

It might seem that many components of this reform package are familiar from past antitrust practice. That is in fact correct. It is correct because—as noted at the outset of this book—many of the weaknesses of current policy have arisen as enforcement practice retreated from areas of prior activity. The Merger Guidelines, for example, have a long history, but those guidelines have gradually become much more permissive. Simply restoring some of their scope and strictness would represent a straightforward step toward improved merger control. Similarly, reliance on the structural presumption would not be so much revolutionary as a restoration of an approach sanctioned by court decisions and supported by economic evidence. Greater attention to exclusionary effects, nonprice consequences, and vertical foreclosure, as well as a sterner treatment of efficiencies and remedies would all be well within the discretion of the agencies, since these are implied by language prohibiting "substantial lessening of competition." In short, this seemingly more expansive merger control proposal resurrects many doctrines and practices that served competition and consumers well in the past and would do so again.

As with any reform proposal, it is fair to ask what the consequences might be. The standard method in economics for predicting the effects of policy is to examine analogous past experiences. That is not possible here since there has been no past effort to initiate such a set of reform proposals. As a result, it might therefore seem impossible to predict the actual effect of reforming merger control as proposed here. But in fact, that is not correct, since in this particular case we know a lot about the outcome. The reason is that over the last forty years we have essentially run the experiment in reverse, and we know how it comes out. Beginning with the Chicago school's skeptical view of antitrust intervention generally and abetted by the narrow view of antitrust implied by increased economic sophistication and promoted by certain interests, we have moved toward an ever-narrower view of antitrust and an ever more accommodating policy toward mergers. We now have a good idea of the results. As documented at the very outset of this monograph, the results of permissiveness have included higher concentration and prices, reduced entry and dynamism, and persistent abnormal profit levels in the U.S. economy. Other researchers have found evidence that the rise in concentration has also reduced innovation, caused wages to stagnate, hindered productivity growth, and enlarged income inequality.

These adverse effects did not have to be. These adverse effects do not have to be. And the reform package detailed herein would ensure that they do not continue. Rather, we can restore a true market economy, one with reduced concentration, greater dynamism, normal profits to firms, competitive prices to consumers, good returns to workers, and strengthened productivity and innovation. This book, it is hoped, provides a roadmap to that destination.

APPENDIX A

Recommendations

Re-establishing the Role of Market Structure: Merger Guidelines and the Structural Presumption

(1) The FTC and DOJ must commit to fully enforcing the market share and concentration standards in the Horizontal Merger Guidelines as written.

(2) The agencies need to make clear that the mergers falling near the thresholds are not in fact subject to significantly looser standards than written, but rather will receive the full degree of scrutiny that the relevant thresholds imply.

(3) The agencies must explicitly endorse the doctrine of a structural presumption in the case of large mergers in high concentration industries. They should use that doctrine to avoid the need for detailed analysis of effects in particular cases, subject only to sharply limited counter-arguments from merging parties.

(4) The agencies should employ a nearly-irrebuttable presumption against mergers resulting in one, two, or three competitors, and a still formidable presumption against those resulting in four or five competitors. Explicit evidence of effects is not necessary.

(5) The agencies need to revise their declaration that mergers below some threshold generally raise no competitive concerns and ordinarily will not be challenged since evidence shows such mergers can in fact be anticompetitive.

(6) The agencies should undertake further statistical analysis of the relevant share and concentration thresholds to ensure that these presumptions conform to the most current and complete evidence.

(7) The agencies need to work towards issuing guidelines on topics in addition to horizontal mergers, topics such as vertical mergers and innovation, in order to provide useful guidance and clarity about their analytical approach to these questions.

(8) The agencies need to develop reliable presumptions wherever feasible and efficient relative to a case-by-case approach. Based on all evidence, these would be useful for addressing claims of merger-related efficiencies and ease of entry into markets.

Rethinking "Plus/Minus" Factors: Efficiencies, Entry Conditions, and Potential Competition

(1) The Merger Guidelines should clearly state that the share and concentration thresholds allow for standard or typical efficiencies and benefits from a merger so that only the most unusual or exceptional or extraordinary claims will be considered on a case-by-case basis. Consideration should be given to setting some minimum degree of efficiencies for case-specific analysis.

(2) The guidelines should make clear that even such extraordinary claims must be verified by evidence from past practice or from documentation prepared in the ordinary course of business well before the merger proposal. This would give little or no weight to claims and reports about prospective efficiencies that have been prepared only for the purpose of a merger justification to the agencies.

(3) The guidelines should make clear that extraordinary claims of efficiencies will be subject to ex post review by the agency. Where the full extent of claimed efficiencies within a two- or three-year period cannot be verified with clear and convincing evidence, the merger will be subject to remedial action by the agency.

(4) The agencies should treat claims of easy entry extremely cautiously since an erroneously accepted claim can undermine a determination of anticompetitive effects and thereby lead to approval of the merger and a lasting increase in market power.

(5) In evaluating claims of easy entry, more weight needs to be put on evidence of past entry and on business considerations favoring future entry than on conceptual arguments about the possibility of entry. If the market shows little sign of past entry, that should be taken as indicative of significant impediments to entry whether or not the specific barriers are identifiable.

(6) The Merger Guidelines must describe more fully the competitive concerns with mergers that create or enhance entry barriers. The discussion should provide examples, types, methods, and specific competitive concerns associated with heightened barriers.

(7) The basic framework for analyzing mergers should not be limited to likely price effects, but rather must define as competitively problematic any merger that materially impedes competition by handicapping or preventing entry, growth, and stronger competition from an actual or potential rival.

(8) The agencies must directly challenge mergers eliminating significant potential competitors to markets. Since the Supreme Court has created an undue burden on such enforcement, this reform might require legislative action.

(9) The agencies need to develop standards for enforcing the doctrine of potential competition. The standards should reflect considerations such as market concentration, the number of significant potential entrants, and relevant distinctions among the latter.

(10) These standards should be included in revised Merger Guidelines and advocated by the agencies to the courts. A determination could be strengthened by, but not ultimately dependent on, documents or past experience or by evidence of the outside firm's effect on the market or its consideration of entry.

Revisiting Other Merger Outcomes: Nonprice Effects, Monopsony, and Remedies

(1) The agencies must set out the distinctive concern and aspects of nonprice effects of mergers and incorporate these considerations in the Merger Guidelines or at least in some alternative policy commentary or guidance.

(2) This guidance likely must be different according to each specific effect, such as quality, variety, and innovation, since the underlying economics and analytical approach for each are different.

(3) The agencies should challenge mergers based on nonprice effects of mergers whenever those are the dominant issue. It is essential to do so in order to restore vitality to these concerns and to persuade the judiciary of their importance.

(4) The discussion of mergers between competing buyers in the Merger Guidelines needs further development with respect to several issues. These include the distinctive features of geographic market definition (e.g., labor mobility), possible entry by new input buyers, and other issues.

(5) While the Merger Guidelines note the distinction between lower input prices due to monopsony power versus lower prices due to reductions in transactions costs and perhaps due to changes in bargaining, operational criteria for these distinctions need to be provided.

(6) Merger policy needs to move expeditiously to catch up with the actual exercise of monopsony power resulting from mergers.

(7) Merger policy needs to challenge anticompetitive mergers rather than settle for remedies in all cases except where circumstances predictably justify the use of remedies. The necessary conditions for remedies should be narrowly construed and specified in policy documents.

(8) Conduct remedies in particular must be avoided except for very unusual cases where merger benefits are large and indisputable, where there is no alternative, and where conditions for their success are fully satisfied. Otherwise, the merger should be challenged.

(9) The agencies need to monitor the outcomes of mergers cleared subject to remedies, impose fines and other penalties for non-compliance with the terms of the remedy, and intervene if necessary after the fact in order to restore market competition.

Reviewing Broader Issues: Vertical Mergers, Common Ownership, and Tech

(1) The near per se legality favoring vertical mergers must be expressly revoked. Vertical Merger Guidelines should be issued detailing the nature of and conditions for such competitive concerns as foreclosure, the elimination of potential competition, and the creation of two-market entry barriers.

(2) Claims that a vertical merger will, or is necessary to, eliminate double marginalization must be tested against the alternative of a contract between parties and against other limitations of the theoretical proposition. Claims of other efficiencies and benefits must be assessed by the same standard as for efficiencies generally: past experience or documentation prior to the proposed merger.

(3) The agencies must aggressively challenge anticompetitive vertical mergers, continuing to develop arguments and evidence that will be sustained in the courts.

(4) The exact foundation, magnitude, and effect of common ownership are matters of research importance since its potential effects are not trivial. These should be urgent matters for investigation by the agencies.

(5) Specific policy actions should await the findings of research and investigations with respect to common ownership.

(6) Because network effects confer lasting advantage, the dominant tech and platform companies should bear the burden of proof to demonstrate that any mergers and acquisitions have demonstrable procompetitive effects.

(7) Where there is any likelihood that a target company's technology might evolve or can be modified to challenge any part of a dominant tech company, an acquisition should be per se illegal. There should be no need for proof that the nascent competitor's business model presently includes such a strategy and no defense due to claims of easy entry or efficiencies.

(8) Consideration should given to a moratorium on all mergers and acquisitions by the large tech companies in order to allow the agencies to develop better methods for analysis. The moratorium period should also be used to launch a specialized digital competition regulator whose mandate complements that of the antitrust authorities.

(9) The use of rules to limit pricing or other terms and conditions that disadvantage hosted independent applications on tech platforms must not be relied upon. Similar to rule-based conduct remedies for mergers, they are easier to avoid than to write, and are often unenforceable. Structural solutions—for example, preventing a tech company from having a financial interest in any hosted application or site—need to be considered instead.

(10) Consideration should be given to dissolving past tech sector mergers when the basis for their approval has proven erroneous and when the merger has instead entrenched and extended the tech company's dominance.

Reforming the Merger Control Process: Retrospectives, Resources, and the Judiciary

(1) The agencies must initiate programs of ex post evaluations of some number of mergers each year. Available resources should be redeployed and additional resources should be provided for these programs. DOJ should be granted data-gathering authority comparable to that of the FTC for these purposes.

(2) Agencies should develop specific purposes for their programs of mergers to be evaluated—to cast light on especially important cases, or to evaluate a particular industry or issue, or to assess overall merger policy. Agencies' programs and choices must be overseen by a neutral party to ensure optimal targeting.

(3) As a condition of their filing and investigation by the agencies, merging companies should be required to produce post-merger data necessary to conduct evaluations of the outcomes.

(4) Resources at the FTC and DOJ for antitrust purposes, and for merger evaluation in particular, must be increased. Merger filing fees should be raised to reflect the substantial costs of investigations, especially of large mergers, and should flow directly into increases in agency budgets.

(5) The agencies should seek methods for conserving on resources necessary for merger control, such as greater reliance on presumptions and more extensive use of retrospectives.

(6) Judicial education in modern mainstream merger analysis is needed in order to ensure decisions reflecting current understanding and standards.

(7) The creation of three-judge panels to hear antitrust proceedings would help improve the quality and consistency of the outcomes of litigation.

APPENDIX B

Comments on the FTC Remedies Study

In 2017 the Federal Trade Commission released a study of its remedy orders between 2006 and 2012.[211] This study received much attention and indeed the FTC deserves much credit for undertaking it. Agencies do not often review the effects and effectiveness of their past policies and practices. It takes time and resources from current activities,[212] and then the results may not be favorable to the agency, posing risks of criticism and worse. It is a sign of good government when an agency does this.

This was the second such study done by the FTC. The first, in 1999, was widely recognized as a milestone and resulted in a number of significant changes in the Commission's divestiture policy.[213] It has now been replicated in a number of other countries that have also assessed their remedies practices.[214] This new FTC study has a number of notable features. It covers many more remedies than the earlier one, and obviously focuses on more recent experiences. The involvement of the Bureau of Economics undoubtedly strengthened the analytic foundations of the work. It forthrightly reports a less than perfect record for some of its remedies. And it uses its review to identify ways of improving remedy policy going forward. This, too, is all much to the credit of the agency.

That said, this study was ultimately uneven. While in some places its methodology and conclusions represented advances over its earlier study, in many places it did no better than before, and occasionally even worse. With

---

211 United States Federal Trade Commission. "The FTC's Merger Remedies 2006-2012" (2017).

212 This study lists 115 people as having contributed in some fashion to the study and the report.

213 United States Federal Trade Commission. "A Study of the Commission's Divestiture Process" (1999).

214 For a listing and review of these other studies, see my book, Mergers, Merger Control, and Remedies, MIT Press, 2015, ch. 8. There also were some weaknesses to the 1999 study, which I discuss below.

growing emphasis on remedies, with advances in methods of analyzing policy, and with many comments and suggestions to the FTC in this proceeding, this study was an opportunity to substantially advance our understanding. Instead, it mostly offered some incremental insights, plus a couple misleading conclusions.

The rest of this commentary elaborates on this mixed assessment of the FTC Report, first with respect to its methodology and then its conclusions.

B.1. Methodology of the FTC Report

To begin, the scope of this study was intended to be broader than the 1999 study. The earlier study examined only divestitures, whereas this new study set out to include conduct remedies as well. Even among the 89 orders covering seven years, this study found too few of the latter to draw any conclusions. That is, of course, hardly the agency's fault, but quite unfortunate since conduct remedies are widely believed to be more frequent in the past ten to fifteen years and have become quite controversial.

This study inexplicably uses three quite different methodologies for assessing the outcomes of the 89 total orders. As shown in Table B.1, for 50 orders (56 percent of the cases), the procedure involved full blown case studies, similar (but not identical, for reasons below) to the 1999 study. For the other 39 orders, no case studies were done at all, but instead the FTC used only considerably less complete information. Of those 39, 15 orders were assessed based simply on questionnaires to outside parties, while the remaining 24 (27 percent) orders in the pharmaceutical industry—were assessed based on nothing more than the FTC's own records of their past actions and monitoring of the markets.

Although I said this was inexplicable, in fact the FTC did offer a rationale for this differential treatment. In the original notice for this study, the FTC declared that, with respect to the questionnaire-based assessments, it had extensive expertise in crafting remedies for mergers in certain industries,[215] and that for the records-based assessments in the pharma sector staff has a great deal of information on divestitures as well as close contact with the monitors appointed in the majority of these orders.[216] From this, the FTC concluded that interviews were unnecessary.

---

215 Federal Register FTC Notice, (January 16, 2015) p. 2424, https://www.ftc.gov/system/files/documents/federal_register_notices/2015/01/1501hsrdivestiturefrn1.pdf.

216 *Ibid.*

It is difficult to be satisfied with the questionnaire procedure, and impossible to be satisfied with the internal records-based assessment procedure. Questionnaires tend to produce formal declarative responses without the subtleties of interviews. They are not well suited to follow-up questions tailored to the circumstances. Records-based assessments are informational closed loops: whatever the agency records and personnel do not know will remain unknown to those who rely on them. Neither of these techniques— certainly not the internal records-based assessments—is a satisfactory basis for the agency's determinations.

More broadly, even the strongest of these methodologies—the case studies—failed to employ modern economic techniques for assessing the impact of policies. Retrospective evaluations of mergers and remedies now routinely use so-called difference-in-differences techniques. Difference in differences compares (say) the price of a product before and after some event (e.g., a merger) or some policy (remedy), netting out changes due to other influences. A remedies study that does not use any such formal techniques to control for other influences, to test for systematic effects, and to compile the experiences does not reflect sound current methodology.

When the FTC outlined this tripartite methodology in the original Notice, I submitted comments that pointed out these concerns and urged instead a consistent and thorough methodology for assessing all the orders.[217] No doubt the costs of doing 89 rather than 50 full blown case studies would be nontrivial. On the other hand, to undertake this study and fail to do the necessary analysis on nearly half of the orders is unfortunate, to say the least—truly a missed opportunity. Worse yet, by failing to use a consistent methodology, the results are not equally strong and certainly not comparable across all subsets of the cases. And worst of all, by failing to use modern analytical techniques, this study fell short of contemporary standards for persuasive research.

In addition to different methodologies, the FTC Report uses different criteria for what it concludes to be a successful remedy order across these different categories. For those 50 fully assessed orders, the Report describes the test as whether competition remained at its premerger level or returned to that level "within...two to three years." By contrast, for the 15 orders assessed using questionnaires, success was defined simply as continued production of the divested product, not whether competition was preserved or restored by the remedy. For the remaining 24 orders arising in the pharmaceutical in-

217 John Kwoka, Comment on the Merger Remedies Study Proposed by the Federal Trade Commission, FTC File No. P143100, March 2015.

dustry, the criteria for success varied even further. For orders addressing cases where both merging parties sold the product, success was again defined as continued production of the product. But for cases of divestiture of pipeline products—those in the development stage—the divestiture was viewed as successful simply if the assets designated for transfer were in fact transferred. This does not even purport to measure survivorship of the assets for any period of time, much less their competitive effects. These varying criteria are summarized in Table B.1.

Even with the 50 orders assessed with case studies, the criterion for success deserves comment. Without explanation, a two- to three-year delay in restoration of competition is viewed as a fully successful remedy, even though much harm may occur in such an interval. Relative to doing nothing, that may seem the better course, but relative to prohibiting the merger altogether, that period represents a true loss of some magnitude.

The Report declared a remedy to be a qualified success if competition were restored but it takes more time than two or three years. But if competition returns in more than three years, it could easily be due to exogenous factors or to endogenous responses within the market, neither of which should be credited to the remedy. This is especially true since the criterion of "more than two or three years" can mean any number of years after the remedy is imposed. For this reason, the agency should have reported more fully on the time period required for a return of competition to those cases it termed "qualified successes."

And finally, the Report describes some of the factors and evidence that went into its determinations of successful remedies. These are all familiar to an economist's assessment, but the process is still pretty opaque. While there is no way that all of the evidence could be put on the public record, there is one important action that the FTC could have and still should do to improve transparency. For these 50 fully analyzed orders, the FTC should release its "scorecard" indicating which ones it judged to be successful and which not. This would not violate confidentiality, but it would help make its conclusions more convincing.

B.2. Conclusions of the FTC Report

Some of the conclusions of the FTC Report were a bit scattered, so it may be useful to pull them together in summary form (see Table B.1). First, for the 50 orders assessed with full case studies and employing the criterion of competition, the FTC reports full "success" in about two-thirds of cases involving horizontal concerns. By adding the cases of "qualified [that is, delayed] success," the Report states that "with respect to the orders examined [more precisely, of this category of orders], more than 80 percent of the Commission's orders maintained or restored competition.[218]

In contrast, the Report devotes a single page to its conclusions with respect to the 15 orders assessed using questionnaires. This may be a reflection of the minimal depth of this method of analysis. Recalling that these were judged "successes" against the lower bar of continued production, the Report states that 39 of a total of 43 products covered by these 15 orders were "successes," which implies a 91 percent "success" rate. The Report does not address the fraction that preserved or restored otherwise lost competition.

The conclusions for the remaining 24 orders are also discussed in a single page in the Report. These orders covered 92 cases in pharmaceuticals, divided as follows: Of 60 cases of product overlaps between the merging companies, 18 cases involved contract manufacturing, so that all that was required was re-assignment of the supply agreement. All of these 18 contracts were in fact re-assigned, leading the Report to declare them "successes." Another 42 product overlap cases involved the need for divesting manufacturing assets. Of these, there were 27 "successful" asset transfers and 15 failures. Finally, all of the 32 cases involving divestiture of product development assets were declared "successes" by virtue of the fact that the transfers in fact occurred, regardless of what ensued. For none of these do we learn anything about the fraction of orders that resulted in the preservation or restoration of competition.

A few additional observations are appropriate.

(1) The report highlighted the rate of success for the 50 orders assessed using case studies. Among the 46 horizontal cases, 66 percent were fully successful (69 percent of all cases in this category). Read differently, however, that implies that in one-third of cases, competition was lost for a minimum of two or three years and perhaps indefinitely. One obvious question is whether this is an acceptable failure rate, that is, whether it satisfies the objective of remedies, or whether it signals the need for more outright enforcement actions against such mergers. Tellingly, after issuance of this report, the incoming (and now) chair of the FTC declared that this failure rate was not acceptable and vowed to implement changes in remedy policy.

(2) The FTC should now further exploit the data and investigate the roots of success or failure of these 50 remedies. Having judged which were successfully resolved, the next step should be to conduct a statistical analy-

---

218 Report, p. 2.

sis of the factors associated with different outcomes.[219] These factors might involve characteristics of the product, the market, the firms, the transaction, and the specific competition problem. That would permit answering such questions as whether the rate of success varies with the size of the firms, or with the heterogeneity of the products, and so forth. A further analysis along these lines could significantly advance understanding of when and where remedies should be used, and when and where they should not, at least not in their present form. These are important questions that can be examined without the need for much if any new data collection, and certainly not another study.

(3) The FTC Report found a substantially lower rate of success about 56 percent of orders—where a divestiture remedy transferred less than the entirety of a business unit. As a result, it stated its "preference" for divestitures of entire business units.[220] This finding is no surprise, however, since the 1999 Study found only a 60 percent success rate measured against the lower bar of asset viability for these kinds of divestitures. That earlier report also recommended against them for that reason.[221] But having already studied these partial-entity divestitures and determined them often to be failures, the obvious question is why the FTC did not follow its own advice but instead persisted in pursuing a flawed strategy. In this Report the FTC asserted that it resorts to partial-entity divestitures only when necessary, but that would seem to mean when necessary to use some kind of remedy instead of challenging the merger. But it is not necessary to use a remedy. Such a high rate of failure nearly half the time—signals instances in which stricter enforcement is called for. The FTC should now face a far heavier burden for resorting to such remedies in the future.

(4) For the other 44 percent of non-case-study orders, the FTC Report simply erred in lowering the standard for success. It is only by declaring a remedy successful if a contract or project that was required to be transferred was in fact transferred, that the Report arrives at a 100 percent success rate for such remedies. In more challenging cases where physical assets needed to be transferred, 64 percent resulted in successful transfer, but in each case, the true percent of cases that preserve or restore competition was strictly lower. This standard was substantively incorrect, and the use of the same terminology invites an exaggerated view of success of remedy policy.

---

219 There is some discussion of this in various places in the Report, but that does not qualify as statistical analysis.

220 Report, pp. 22, 32.

221 United States Federal Trade Commission, "The FTC's Merger Remedies 2006-2012: A Report of the Bureaus of Competition and Economics," pp. 11-12 (2017).

On the other hand, the FTC should be commended for its Best Practices section, which is devoted to extracting lessons from its analysis of remedial orders. While some stronger conclusions might have been warranted, this is a valuable part of the FTC Report.

B.3 Some Recommendations

The FTC deserves credit for putting itself under a microscope and acknowledging some instances in which its policies have not worked. But the study it undertook was ultimately uneven and incomplete, and indeed sometimes flawed in its methodology. There are, however, a number of actions that the FTC could still undertake that will advance understanding about the effects and effectiveness of its remedy policies.

First and foremost, the FTC should complete its job. It should immediately return to the 39 orders where it relied on questionnaires and internal reports and undertake the necessary full case studies. Also, for these 39 orders, it should evaluate the success of the remedy by the correct standard of whether it preserved or restored the competition lost due to the merger and only use the term "success" for this standard. This further work will take full advantage of what has already been done. It will ask and answer the right question about remedies. And it will not require waiting another eighteen years to learn the answers.

Apart from that, there are other ways in which the FTC can exploit the data it already has compiled. These include at least the following:

(1) *The FTC should report data on the delays it observed in restoring competition for those remedies that did not do so immediately. For those described as successes, it would be useful to know how many took fully three years, for example, and for those with greater delays "qualified success", what were the frequencies of long delays (e.g., five or more years).*

(2) *The FTC should release a scorecard of the 50 orders assessed with case studies, with an indication of those that were full successes vs. "qualified [delayed] successes" vs. failures.*

(3) The FTC should compile further information on the firm, market, and product characteristics associated with the 50 orders and conduct a statistical analysis of the correlates of success vs. failure. The results of the analysis should be made public so as to permit—indeed, facilitate—discussion of how best to improve remedy policy.

TABLE B.1

Summary of FTC Remedies Study

Number of Orders	Method of Analysis	Criterion for "Success"	Outcome
50	Case study	"Success" if competition restored in 2 to 3 years	69% of all 50 remedies
		"Qualified success" if competition restored in more than 2 to 3 years	14% of all 50 remedies
			17% of 50 remedies failed
15	Questionnaires	"Success" if production of divested product continued	91% "Success"
			9% failed
24	Agency records	"Success" if either production continued, or asset actually transferred	75% of total successful
			25% failed

APPENDIX C

Bibliography

Anglen, Robert. *Albertsons buys back stores feds forced it to sell*, THE REPUBLIC, Nov. 25, 2015.

Aghion, Philippe, Nick Bloom, Richard Blundell, Rachel Griffith & Peter Howitt. *Competition and Innovation: An Inverted-U Relationship*, 120 QUARTERLY JOURNAL OF ECONOMICS 2, 701-728 (2005).

Aguirregabiri, Victor & Chun-Yu Ho. *Hub-and-Spoke Networks and Entry Deterrence*, 28 INTERNATIONAL JOURNAL OF INDUSTRIAL ORGANIZATION 4 (2010).

Arlen, Gary. *DOJ, FTC Officials Spar over Roles in Antitrust Reviews*, MULTICHANNEL NEWS, March 21, 2019.

Ashenfeler, Orley, Daniel Hoskens & Matthew Weinberg. *Price Effects of a Large Manufacturing Merger: A Case Study of Maytag-Whirlpool*, 5 AMERICAN ECONOMIC JOURNAL: ECONOMIC POLICY 2013, 1, 239–261 (2013).

Ashenfelter, Orley & Alan Krueger. *Theory and Evidence on Employer Collusion in the Franchise Sector*, (NBER, Working Paper No. 24831, 2018).

Autor, David, David Dorn, Lawrence Katz, Christina Patterson & John Van Reenen. *Concentrating on the Fall of Labor Share*, 107 AMERICAN ECONOMIC REVIEW 5, 180-85, (2017).

Azar, Jose, Martin Schmalz & Isabel Tecu. *Anticompetitive Effects of Common Ownership*, 73 JOURNAL OF FINANCE, 1513-1565 (2018).

Backus, Matthew, Christopher Conlon & Michael Sinkinso. *The Common Ownership Hypothesis: Theory and Evidence*, BROOKINGS (January 2019).

Baker, Jonathan. THE ANTITRUST PARADIGM: RESTORING A COMPETITIVE ECONOMY. (Harvard University Press, 2019).

Baker, Jonathan. *The Problem with Baker Hughes and Syufy: On the Role of Entry in Merger Analysis*, ANTITRUST LAW JOURNAL, (1997).

Baker, Jonathan. *Exclusion as a Core Competition Concern*, 88 ANTITRUST LAW JOURNAL, 527-589 (2013).

Baker, Jonathan. *Market Power in the U.S. Economy Today*, WASHINGTON CENTER FOR EQUITABLE GROWTH, (March 20, 2017), https://equitablegrowth.org/market-power-in-the-u-s-economy-today/.

Baker, Jonathan & Fiona Scott Morton. *Antitrust Enforcement Against Platform MFNs*, 127 YALE LAW JOURNAL, 2176-2202 (2018).

Baker, Jonathan & Carl Shapiro. *Reinvigorating Horizontal Merger Enforcement*, in HOW THE CHICAGO SCHOOL OVERSHOT THE MARK, (R. Pitofsky, ed., Oxford, 2008).

Balan, David. *A Retrospective Analysis of the Clinical Quality Effects of the Acquisition of Highland Park Hospital by Evanston Northwestern Healthcare*, 18 INTERNATIONAL JOURNAL OF THE ECONOMICS OF BUSINESS 1, 45-64 (2010).

Bartz, Diane. *Justice Department Investigates Beer Industry Anticompetition Accusations*, REUTERS, Oct. 12, 2015.

Berman, Dennis. *to Assess 2007 M&A Activity*, WALL STREET JOURNAL, Jan. 16, 2007.

Berry, Steven T. *Estimating a Model of Entry in the Airline Industry*, 60 ECONOMETRICA, 889-917, (1992).

Blonigen, Bruce & Justin Pierce, *Evidence for the Effects of Mergers on Market Power and Efficiency,* Finance and Economics Discussion Series 2016-082. Washington: Board of Governors of The Federal Reserve System, 2016.

Bork, Robert. THE ANTITRUST PARADOX: A POLICY AT WAR WITH ITSELF (1978).

Bose, Nandita & Jeffrey Dustin. *Amazon Admits It Uses Aggregated Seller Data to Help Business*, REUTERS, Nov. 13, 2019.

Carlton, Dennis. *Why We Need to Measure the Effect of Merger Policy and How to Do It*, 5 COMPETITION POLICY INTERNATIONAL (2009).

Carstensen, Peter. COMPETITION POLICY AND THE CONTROL OF BUYER POWER, Edwin Elgar, 2017.

Chancellor of the Exchequer, UK. Unlocking Digital Competition: Report of the Expert Panel (March 2019).

Christofferson, Scott A., Robert S. McNish & Diane L. Sias. *Where Mergers Go Wrong*, MCKINSEY QUARTERLY, 1–6, (2004).

Ciliberto, Federico & Jonathan Williams. "Limited Access to Airport Facilities and Market Power in the Airline Industry," JOURNAL OF LAW AND ECONOMICS, August 2010.

Coate, Malcolm. *The Merger Review Process at the Federal Trade Commission from 1989 to 2016* (February 28, 2018), SSRN: https://ssrn.com/abstract=2955987.

Council of Economic Advisers. *The Benefits of Competition and Indicators of Market Power,* (April 2016).

Council of Economic Advisors. *Labor Market Monopsony: Trends, Consequences and Policy Responses,* (October 2016).

Covert, Adrian. *Facebook Buys WhatsApp for $19 Billion*, CNN TECH, Feb. 19, 2014.

Craig, Stuart, Matthew Grennan & Ashley Swanson. *Mergers and Marginal Costs: New Evidence on Hospital Buyer Power* (NBER, Working Paper No. 24926, August 2018).

Cunningham, Colleen, Florian Ederer & Song Ma. *Killer Acquisitions*, (2018). SSRN: https://papers.ssrn.com/sol3/papers.cfm?abstract_id=3241707.

Dalkir, Serdar & Frederick Warren-Boulton. *Prices, Market Definition, and the Effects of Merger: Staples-Office Depot*, in THE ANTITRUST REVOLUTION (J. Kwoka & L. White, eds., 6th edition 2014).

Decker, Ryan, John Haltiwanger, Ron Jarmin & Javier Miranda. *The Role of Entrepreneurship in US Job Creation and Economic Dynamism*, 28 JOURNAL OF ECONOMIC PERSPECTIVES 3, 3-24 (2014).

DeGraba, Patrick & Gregory Rosston. *The Proposed Merger of AT&T and T-Mobile*, in THE ANTITRUST REVOLUTION (J. Kwoka & L. White, eds., 6th edition, 2014).

De Loecker, Jan & Jan Eeckhout. *The Rise of Market Power and the Macroeconomic Implications* (NBER, Working Paper No. 23687, 2017).

Delrahim, Makin. Modernizing the Merger Review Process, Remarks at the Global Antitrust Forum, (Sept. 25, 2018).

Doidge, Craig, Kathleen Kahle, G. Andrew Karolyi & Rene Stulz. *Eclipse of the Public Corporation or Eclipse of the Public Markets?* (NBER, Working Paper No. 24265; 2018).

Dustin, Jeffrey. *JetBlue to charge for checked bags in new airfare class*, REUTERS, Nov. 19, 2014.

Elhauge, Einer. *Horizontal Shareholding*, 129 HARVARD LAW REVIEW 5, 1267-1317 (2016).

Farrell, Joseph & Mark Chicu. *Pharmaceutical Patents and Pay for Delay: Actavis*, in THE ANTITRUST REVOLUTION (John Kwoka & Lawrence White, eds., 7th edition, 2019).

Farrell, Joseph & John Kwoka. *Resetting Merger Policy in the New Administration*, 4 CONCURRENCES (2016).

Fauver, Jennifer & Subramaniam Ramanarayanan. *Challenges for Economic Analysis of Mergers Between Potential Competitors: Steris and Synergy*, 30 ANTITRUST (2016).

Federico, Giulio, Gregor Langus & Tommaso Valetti. *Horizontal Mergers and Product Innovation*, 59 INTERNATIONAL JOURNAL OF INDUSTRIAL ORGANIZATION C, 1-23 (2018).

Gilbert, Rich. INNOVATION MATTERS: COMPETITION POLICY FOR THE HIGH TECHNOLOGY ECONOMY, MIT Press, forthcoming.

Gilbert, Rich & Steven Sunshine. *Incorporating Dynamic Efficiency Concerns in Merger Analysis: The Use of Innovation Markets*, 63 ANTITRUST LAW JOURNAL 2, 569-601 (1995).

Gilje, Erik, Todd A. Gormley & Doron Levit. *The Rise of Common Ownership* (University of Pennsylvania and Washington University in St. Louis, Working Paper, 2018).

Ginsburg, Douglas & Joshua Wright. *Philadelphia National Bank: Bad Economics, Bad Law, Good Riddance*, 80 ANTITRUST LAW JOURNAL 2 (2015).

Grullon, Gustavo, Yelena Larkin & Roni Michaely. *Are U.S. Industries Becoming More Concentrated?* 23 REVIEW OF FINANCE 4, 697–743, 2019.

Hagey, Keach & Vivien Ngo. *How Google Edged Out Rivals and Built the World's Dominant Ad Machine*, WALL STREET JOURNAL, Nov. 7, 2019.

Hemphill, Scott & Nancy L. Rose. *Mergers That Harm Sellers*, 127 YALE LAW JOURNAL 7, 1742-2203 (2018).

Israel, Mark, Bryan Keating, Daniel Rubinfeld & Robert Willig, *The Delta-Northwest Merger: Consumer Benefits from Airline Network Effects*, in THE ANTITRUST REVOLUTION, (Kwoka & White, eds., 6th edition 2014).

Jarsulic, Marc, Ethan Gurwitz & Andrew Schwartz. *Toward a Robust Competition Policy*, CENTER FOR AMERICAN PROGRESS, (April 3, 2019), https://www.americanprogress.org/issues/economy/reports/2019/04/03/467613/toward-robust-competition-policy/.

Kendall, Brent. *As Mergers Multiply, U.S. Antitrust Cops Raise Their Game*, WALL STREET JOURNAL, July 2, 2015.

Kendall, Brent & Jacqueline Palank. *How the FTC'S Hertz Antitrust Fix Went Flat*, WALL STREET JOURNAL, Dec. 8, 2013.

Kennedy, Pauline, Daniel O'Brien, Minjae Song & Keith Waehrer. *The Competitive Effects of Common Ownership: Economic Foundations and Empirical Evidence*, SSRN: https://ssrn.com/abstract=3008331.

Klein, Joel. The Importance of Antitrust Enforcement in the New Economy, Address to the New York State Bar Assn. (January 29, 1998).

Kosman, Josh. *Facebook Boasted of Buying Instagram to Kill the Competition*, NEW YORK POST, Feb. 26, 2019.

Kovacic, William. *Assessing the Quality of Competition Policy: The Case of Horizontal Merger Enforcement*, 5 COMPETITION POLICY INTERNATIONAL (2009).

Krueger, Alan & Orley Ashenfelter. *Theory and Evidence on Employer Collusion in the Franchise Sector* (NBER, Working Paper No. 24831, 2018).

Kwoka, John. *Non-Incumbent Competition: Mergers Involving Constraining and Prospective Competitors*, 52 Case W. Res. L. Rev., 173-209 (2001).

Kwoka, John. MERGERS, MERGER CONTROL AND REMEDIES: A RETROSPECTIVE ANALYSIS OF U.S. POLICY (MIT Press, 2015).

Kwoka, John. *The Changing Nature of Efficiencies in Mergers and Merger Analysis*, 60 ANTITRUST BULLETIN 3, 231-249, (2015).

Kwoka, John. *One and a Half Cheers for the FTC Remedies Study*, SSRN (February 1, 2017), https://ssrn.com/abstract=3112689.

Kwoka, John. *Merger Remedies: An Incentives/Constraints Framework*, 62 ANTITRUST BULLETIN 2, 367-381 (2017).

Kwoka, John. *The Structural Presumption and Safe Harbor in Merger Review: False Positives or Unwarranted Concerns?* 82 ANTITRUST LAW JOURNAL 1, (2017).

Kwoka, John. *The Effects of Mergers on Innovation: Economic Framework and Empirical Evidence,"* in THE ROLES OF INNOVATION IN COMPETITION LAW ANALYSIS, (Edgar Elger, 2018).

Kwoka, John. *Masquerading as Merger Control: The U.S. Department of Justice Settlement with Sprint and T-Mobile*, AMERICAN ANTITRUST INSTITUTE (August 2019) https://www.antitrustinstitute.org/wp-content/uploads/2019/08/Kwoka_Sprint-TMobile-Settlenent_8.21.19_F.pdf.

Kwoka, John. *Conduct Remedies, with 2020 Hindsight: Have We Learned Anything in the Last Decade?*, CPI ANTITRUST CHRONICLE, April 2020, Vol. 1(1), pp. 12-17.

Kwoka, John. *The Promise and Perils of Conduct Remedies in Merger Review*, forthcoming.

Kwoka, John, Phillippe Alepin & Kevin Hearle. *From the Fringe to the Forefront: Low-Cost Carriers and Airline Price Determination*, 48 REVIEW OF INDUSTRIAL ORGANIZATION 3, (2016).

Kwoka, John & Shawn Kilpatrick. *Nonprice Effects of Mergers*, 63 ANTITRUST BULLETIN 2, 169-182 (2018).

Kwoka, John & Evgenia Shumilkina. *The Price Effect of Eliminating Potential Competition: Evidence from an Airline Merger*, 58 JOURNAL OF INDUSTRIAL ECONOMICS 4, (2010).

Kwoka, John & Margaret Slade. *Second Thoughts on Double Marginalization*, SSRN (Sept. 13, 2019), https://papers.ssrn.com/sol3/papers.cfm?abstract_id=3452207.

Le, Huubinh. *An Empirical Analysis of the Price and Output Effects of the Southwest/AirTran Merger*, 17 COMPETITION AND REGULATION IN NETWORK INDUSTRIES, 3-4, 226-240, (2016).

Lohr, Steve & Erin Griffith. *With Big Tech in Their Paths, Start-Ups Turn to Business Markets*, NEW YORK TIMES, Nov. 22, 2019.

Mackintosh, James. *The Fed Worries about Corporate Monopolies, Investors Should Just Buy Them*, WALL STREET JOURNAL, Aug. 24, 2018.

Marinescu, Ioana & Herbert Hovencamp. *Anticompetitive Mergers in Labor Markets*, FACULTY SCHOLARSHIP AT PENN LAW, 1031-1063 (2019).

Marx, Leslie & Greg Shaffer. *Slotting Allowances and Scarce Shelf Space*, 19 JOURNAL OF ECONOMICS AND MANAGEMENT STRATEGY 3, 575-603 (2010).

Mickle, Tripp. *Craft Brewers Take Issue with AB Inbev Distribution Plan*, WALL STREET JOURNAL, Dec. 5, 2015.

Moss, Diana. *Delivering the Benefits? Efficiencies and Airline Mergers*, AMERICAN ANTITRUST INSTITUTE, (November 21, 2013), SSRN: https://ssrn.com/abstract=2547673.

Moss, Diana. *The Record of Weak U.S. Merger Enforcement in Big Tech*, AMERICAN ANTITRUST INSTITUTE, 2019.

Moss, Diana. "The Record of Weak U.S. Merger Enforcement in Big Tech," AMERICAN ANTITRUST INSTITUTE, July 2019.

Moss, Diana & John Kwoka. *Behavioral Merger Remedies: Evaluation and Implications for Antitrust Enforcement*, 57 ANTITRUST BULLETIN 4, 979-1011 (2012).

Motta, Massimo & E. Tarantino. *The Effect of Horizontal Mergers When Firms Compete in Prices and Investments*, Department of Economics and Business, Universitat Pompeu Fabra, Economics Working Paper No. 1579, 2017.

Mullins, Brody, Rolfe Winkler & Brent Kendall. *Inside the FTC Probe of Google*, WALL STREET JOURNAL, Mar. 19, 2015.

Naidu, Suresh, Eric Posner & E. Glen Weyl. *Antitrust Remedies for Labor Market Power*, 132 HARVARD LAW REVIEW, 549-600 (2018).

OECD Roundtable, *Impact Evaluation of Merger Decisions* (2014), http://www.oecd.org/daf/competition/Impactevaluationofmergerdecisions2011.pdf.

Open Markets Institute. *America's Concentration Crisis*, (Nov. 2018), https://concentrationcrisis.openmarketsinstitute.org.

Philippon, Thomas. THE GREAT REVERSAL: HOW AMERICA GAVE UP ON FREE MARKETS. (Harvard University Press, 2019).

Posner, Richard & C. Scott Hemphill, *Philadelphia National Bank at 50: An Interview with Richard Posner*, 80 ANTITRUST LAW JOURNAL, 205-218 (2015).

Ravenscraft, David J. & Curtis L. Wagner. *The Role of the FTC's Line of Business Data in Testing and Expanding the Theory of the Firm*, 34 THE JOURNAL OF LAW & ECONOMICS 2, 703–39 (1991).

Reder, Melvin. *Chicago Economics: Permanence and Change*, JOURNAL OF ECONOMIC LITERATURE, 1-38 (1982).

Rey, Patrick & Jean Tirole. "A Primer on Foreclosure," in HANDBOOK OF INDUSTRIAL ORGANIZATION (M. Armstrong & R. Porter eds., 2006).

Rogerson, William. *A Vertical Merger in the Video Programming and Distribution Industry: Comcast-NBCU*, in THE ANTITRUST REVOLUTION, (J. Kwoka & L. White, eds., 6th edition 2014).

Rossi-Hansberg, Esteban, Pierre-Daniel Sarte, and Nicholas Trachter, "Diverging Trends in National and Local Concentration," April 2019.

Salinger, Michael, Pauline Ippolito & Joel Schrag. *Economics at the FTC: Pharmaceutical Patent Dispute Settlements and Behavioral Economics*, 31 REVIEW OF INDUSTRIAL ORGANIZATION, 85-105 (2007).

Salop, Steven & David Culley. *Potential Competitive Effects of Vertical Mergers: A How-To Guide for Practitioners* (December 8, 2014) SSRN: https://ssrn.com/abstract=2522179.

Salop Steven. *The Evolution and Vitality of Merger Presumptions: A Decision-Theoretic Approach*, 80 ANTITRUST LAW JOURNAL (2015).

Salop, Steven. *Modifying Merger Consent Decrees to Improve Merger Enforcement Policy*, 31 ANTITRUST 1, 15-20 (2016).

Salop, Steven. *Reinvigorating Vertical Merger Enforcement*, 127 YALE LAW JOURNAL 7, 1742-2203 (2018).

Scherer, F.M. *The Welfare Economics of Product Variety: An Application to the Ready-to-Eat Cereal Industry*, 28 JOURNAL OF INDUSTRIAL ECONOMICS 2, 113-13, (1979).

Shambaugh, Jay, Ryan Nunn, Audrey Breitwieser, Patrick Lu & Becca Portman. *16 Facts about Competition and Dynamism*, BROOKINGS, (June 2018), https://www.brookings.edu/research/the-state-of-competition-and-dynamism-facts-about-concentration-start-ups-and-related-policies/.

Shapiro, Carl. *Mergers with Differentiated Products*, 10 ANTITRUST, 23-30 (Spring 1996).

Shapiro, Carl. *Antitrust in an Age of Populism*, 61 INTERNATIONAL JOURNAL OF INDUSTRIAL ORGANIZATION, 2018.

Shapiro, Carl. *Protecting Competition in the American Economy: Merger Control, Tech Titans, Labor Markets*, 33 JOURNAL OF ECONOMIC PERSPECTIVES 3, 69-93 (2019).

Stellin, Susan. *Seeking a Place at Airports*, NEW YORK TIMES, Jan. 25, 2010.

Stigler Committee on Digital Platforms. Report (May 2019).

Stutz, Randy. *The Evolving Antitrust Treatment of Labor Market Restraints: From Theory to Practice*, AMERICAN ANTITRUST INSTITUTE, (July 31, 2018).

Summers, Adam. *Occupational Licensing*, REASON FOUNDATION (August 1, 2007), https://reason.org/policy-study/occupational-licensing-ranking/.

TechCrunch. *Facebook to Acquire Instagram for $19 Billion*, April 2012.

Tepper, Jonathan. THE MYTH OF CAPITALISM: MONOPOLIES AND THE DEATH OF COMPETITION. (Wiley, 2019).

Tirole, Jean. THE THEORY OF INDUSTRIAL ORGANIZATION, MIT

Press (1988).

Tirole, Jean. *A Nobel-Prize Winning Economist's Guide to Taming Tech Monopolies*, 2018.

Topper, Michael, Stanley Watt & Marshall Yan. *Google-ITA: Creating a New Flight Search Competitor*, in THE ANTITRUST REVOLUTION, (J. Kwoka & L. White, eds., 6th edition, 2014).

Varney, Christine. An Update on the Review of the Merger Guidelines, Remarks as Prepared for the Horizontal Merger Guidelines Review Project's Final Workshop (Jan. 26, 2010), https://www.ftc.gov/sites/default/files/documents/public_events/horizontal-merger-guidelines-review-project/100126transcript.pdf.

White, Lawrence. *Why Isn't "Deterrence" Included in the Measurements of Antitrust "Enforcement"?*, CPI ANTITRUST CHRONICLE, Nov. 2019, Vol. 2(2), pp. 66-70.

Wollman, Thomas. *Stealth Consolidation: Evidence from an Amendment to the Hart-Scott-Rodino Act*, 1 AER INSIGHTS, 77-94, (2019).

Printed in Great Britain
by Amazon

67353160R00092